The San Diego
WILD ANIMAL PARK

By KAREN E. WORLEY
Publications Department,
Zoological Society of San Diego

Photography by
RON GARRISON, KEN KELLEY,
F. D. SCHMIDT, DAVID GATLEY, AND KEN BOHN
Visual Services Department,
Zoological Society of San Diego

Design by
WARNER DESIGN ASSOCIATES
San Diego, California

Printing by
ANDERSON LITHOGRAPH
Commerce, California

Copyright©2000 by the Zoological Society of San Diego, P.O. Box 120551, San Diego, CA 92112-0551. First Printing.
ISBN 0-911461-17-5. Library of Congress Card Number 00-108003.

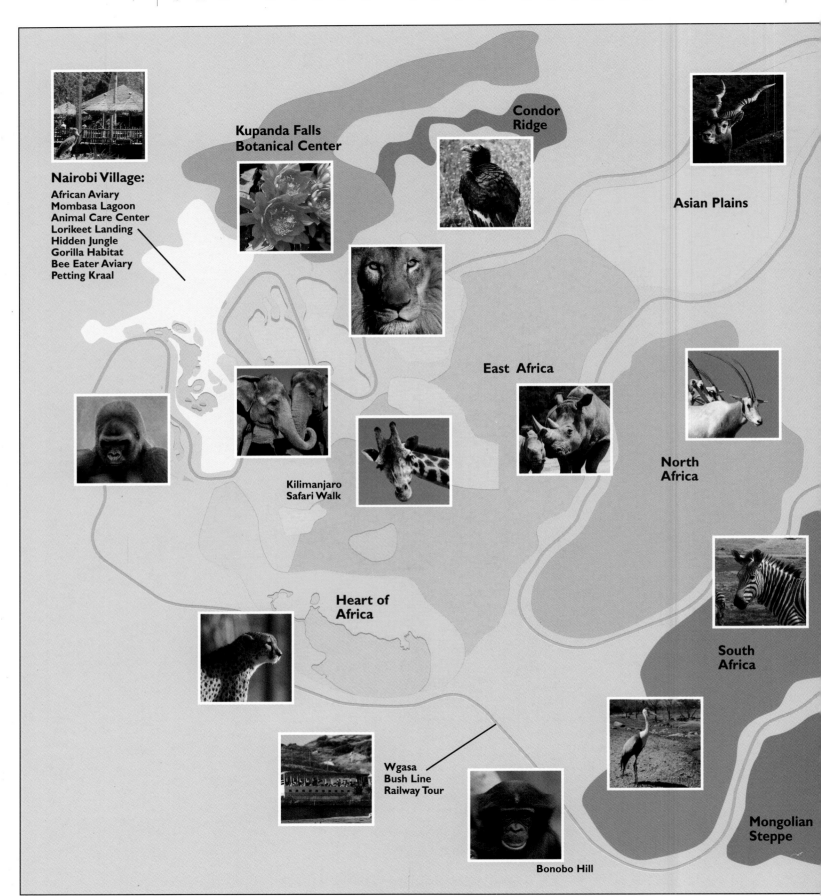

**Kupanda Falls
Botanical Center**

**Condor
Ridge**

Asian Plains

Nairobi Village:

**African Aviary
Mombasa Lagoon
Animal Care Center
Lorikeet Landing
Hidden Jungle
Gorilla Habitat
Bee Eater Aviary
Petting Kraal**

East Africa

**Kilimanjaro
Safari Walk**

**North
Africa**

**Heart of
Africa**

**South
Africa**

**Wgasa
Bush Line
Railway Tour**

**Mongolian
Steppe**

Bonobo Hill

CONTENTS

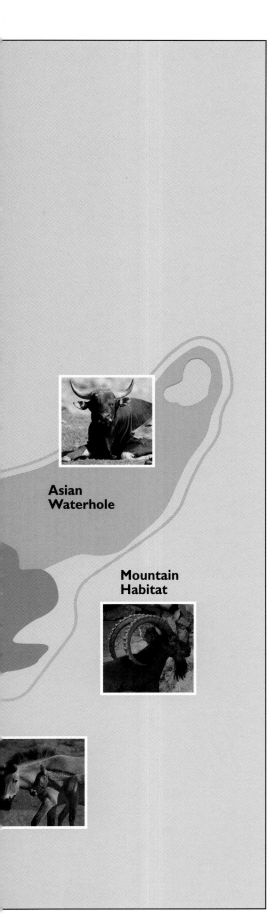

Asian Waterhole

Mountain Habitat

The Wild Animal Park's wide open spaces provide a unique refuge for wildlife.

Welcome to the San Diego Wild Animal Park!

When the San Diego Wild Animal Park was formally dedicated on May 9, 1972, the statement on the dedication plaque expressed the Park's guiding purpose: "Join us here...to contemplate the wild animals of the world and nature's wilderness...to strengthen a commitment to wildlife conservation throughout the world, and to strive toward man's own survival through the preservation of nature." By devoting itself to this purpose, the Wild Animal Park has become one of the most distinctive and successful wildlife preserves in the world. ❧ Spread across the hills of San Pasqual Valley, 30 miles northeast of downtown San Diego, the Park is one of the facilities maintained by the not-for-profit Zoological Society of San Diego. The Park encompasses a total of 1,800 acres, 700 of which have been developed, and several hundred of the remaining acres have been permanently set aside as a native species reserve. The Wild Animal Park provides a unique opportunity to view a remarkable diversity of animals and provides unparalleled family entertainment. Its primary goal has always been to create a naturalistic haven for wildlife that can support wild populations and help to save endangered species.

Thatched roofs and open-air markets in Nairobi Village.

A little bit of Africa in the San Pasqual Valley.

Dr. Schroeder (far left) discusses plans for the Wild Animal Park with San Diego City Council members.

Dr. Schroeder's Vision

Paving the way to the Park.

The Wild Animal Park was the creation of Dr. Charles Schroeder, the Zoological Society's executive director from 1954 to 1972, a tenacious, dedicated, and far-sighted man who had great dreams for the Zoological Society of San Diego. By the mid-1950s, he saw that many exotic species were already becoming scarce, due to the demands of an ever-increasing human population and transportation innovations that made it easier for collectors to travel the globe in search of wild animals. Dr. Schroeder had the foresight to realize that extinctions would accelerate unless zoos began conserving animals, instead of taking them from the wild. 🐾 He first envisioned the Wild Animal Park as a back-country facility to breed animals for the San Diego Zoo and other zoos, creating self-sustaining animal populations. He was convinced that a large auxiliary facility was needed outside the downtown area that could house sizeable breeding groups. In 1962, Dr. Schroeder's search turned up a large parcel of land in the San Pasqual Valley that he considered an ideal site. His challenge then was to convince the community and Zoological Society supporters to go ahead with the ambitious project and raise the money for construction. 🐾 Even his most ardent supporters had difficulty visualizing great things for this sagebrush-covered terrain, but Dr. Schroeder had a clear vision of what the land could become in time. He conveyed that enthusiasm to the Zoological Society's board of trustees, and the board approved the new facility in 1969.

The Park Takes Shape

Dr. Schroeder knew that the San Pasqual Valley landscape would have to be adapted to the needs of exotic wildlife species and the visitors that wished to see them, without compromising the sense of security that, for many animals, is essential to sustained breeding success. This eliminated the concept of a "drive-through safari park." Instead, after examining a variety of transportation systems, the study committee chose an electric monorail system that runs silently on rubber wheels and is nonpolluting. Zoological Society staff members also realized that close-up observation of the animals would bring in visitors, perhaps making the new park a tourist attraction that could eventually become self-supporting. Thus, Nairobi Village was added to the plans, a central public area designed to look like an African village. Its design was developed from drawings that Charles Faust, the Society's graphic designer at the time, sketched in the field on a trip to Africa.

Eager to proceed, Dr. Schroeder took markers out to the site and began staking out the railway route himself.

8

A sketch of the proposed Nairobi Village by graphic designer Charles Faust.

Animals arrived at the Park long before construction was finished and lived in their temporarily fenced field enclosures.

The path to gorillas.

With each year, the Wild Animal Park becomes more lush and beautiful.

A final, crucial hurdle was cleared in 1970, when San Diego voters approved a $6 million private bond proposal to provide funding to build Nairobi Village and install the monorail system. The Park was now on its way. Soon, the Kilimanjaro Safari Walk was added, so that visitors could stroll past magnificent animals like elephants and tigers for a more intimate experience. The Village and the Safari Walk were designed to compliment the "safari" experience of viewing exotic and endangered wildlife species in their expansive field exhibits from the monorail. ⅋ The Wild Animal Park has continued this two-fold approach over the years, with a western lowland gorilla exhibit, three animal show areas, the Hidden Jungle greenhouse, the Lorikeet Landing bird encounter, a variety of walk-through botanical gardens, the Heart of Africa experience, and Condor Ridge all complimenting the monorail adventure, which is now known as the Wgasa Bush Line Railway. ⅋ The Park's long-term goal of becoming self-supporting has been met, and today more than 1.7 million guests visit the Wild Animal Park each year to enjoy its unique atmosphere and the remarkable diversity of wildlife that calls it home.

Safari means "to travel" in Swahili, and visitors to the Wild Animal Park find themselves on a singular journey.

The addaxes *Addax nasomaculatus* began reproducing before the Park was open to the public.

A mother cheetah *Acinonyx jubatus* and her cubs in the early days of the Wild Animal Park.

A Unique Collection for a Unique Park

The first Arabian oryxes *Oryx leucoryx* arrived at the Park soon after it opened, as part of the World Herd brought into captivity to save the species.

In 1969, Dr. James Dolan, Jr., at that time the Zoo's associate curator of birds, was given the exciting and challenging task of building the Park's animal collection from scratch. "We concentrated heavily on acquiring hoofed stock, especially endangered species, because the Park's terrain and climate are geared to that type of animal," said Dr. Dolan, who is now the Zoological Society's director of collections. "We also designed exhibits that were large enough to allow for herds of up to 60 to 70 individuals of the same species." 🦎 As the animals arrived at the still-developing Park, they were housed in holding areas until their exhibits could be completed. Some of the species thriving at the Wild Animal Park since the beginning are Arabian oryxes, South African cheetahs, Formosan sika deer, southern white rhinos, slender-horned gazelles, addaxes, Grevy's zebras, axis deer, and Burmese thamins.

Momentous occasion: Wild Animal Park staff members and Dr. Ian Player of South Africa release the first southern white rhinos *Ceratotherium simum simum* into their field enclosure.

King of the hill: The Wild Animal Park has had great success with southern white rhino reproduction.

One of the many highlights of those early days was the arrival of 20 southern white rhinoceroses from South Africa in 1971. They arrived individually in enormous wooden crates, which were placed on flatbed trucks and driven into the field exhibit that would be their new home. When the staff opened the crates and the magnificent rhinos came dashing out, everyone cheered. At that time, there were only about 1,000 southern white rhinos left in the wild, and the Park had high hopes of successful captive breeding. Those hopes have been more than realized in the years since then, with the births of more than 85 southern white rhinos. ❧ The Park's achievement, along with the work of many other facilities worldwide, has contributed to increasing the southern white rhino population to more than 8,500 today. The species still remains threatened in the wild, but with the Wild Animal Park's help, it has taken a step back from the brink of extinction.

What's the password?
A group of water
buffalo *Bubalus arnee
f. bubalis* unconcernedly
block the path.

Establishing Territories

Grevy's zebra *Equus grevyi*

Dr. Dolan needed to determine the population mix of different species that would live inside the five main field exhibit areas. His decisions were based primarily on the geographic region the animals came from in the wild and his own knowledge of which species might peacefully coexist. He pointed out that "The old zoo concepts for managing large animal species had to be put aside and new methods for their husbandry undertaken, if long-term, self-sustaining populations were to be established as safeguards against extinction. Such a goal could not hope to achieve success where only two or three individuals of a given species could be accommodated. Genetic diversity would be greatly reduced, which could ultimately lead to the collapse of the entire project." ❧ Through daily observations, the Park's field keepers learned to sense which animals didn't fare well in close proximity to other species. Adjustments were made, some species were moved to other areas, and some additional, smaller field enclosures were created for particularly shy or aggressive species that preferred their own company. The Grevy's zebras, for example, started out in the East Africa exhibit, but they were so aggressive toward other species that it was clear they needed their own space.

Mixed company: different species in the East Africa enclosure.

Room to grow: a herd of addra gazelles *Gazella dama ruficollis.*

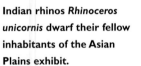

Indian rhinos *Rhinoceros unicornis* **dwarf their fellow inhabitants of the Asian Plains exhibit.**

Once a good balance was reached, the animal groups in each field exhibit were allowed to claim and protect their own territories and establish their own hierarchies, much as they would in the wild. With changes to the mix of species over the years, this natural process has continued as certain species are moved and new ones are introduced. The five main exhibits still largely retain their geographical context, but a few species in them may seem out of place. ❧ The needs of the animals are always the first consideration, and because of factors like space or temperament, you may occasionally find a South African species in an East African exhibit. Ultimately, confusing the geography a bit is worthwhile if the animals are content.

Something for every-
one: Uganda giraffes
*Giraffa camelopardalis
rothschildi.*

Safe and sound: Many species of deer and antelope "tuck" their babies into thickets or among rocks to hide them during the day, as the mother of this nilgai *Boselaphus tragocamelus* calf has done at the Park.

An exuberant Uganda giraffe calf kicks up its heels.

Acting Naturally

From the beginning, the Wild Animal Park staff was concerned about the quality of the animals' environment. They sought ways to create exhibits that catered as much as possible to the natural needs of each species and their potential range of behaviors. As general curator Larry Killmar pointed out, there are some subtle things that make an animal feel at home and, as a result, more likely to reproduce. "One thing was to provide tall feeder poles upon which to hang vegetation for natural browsers like giraffes, elands, and kudus. They can adjust and eat browse that's lying on the ground, but they're much happier reaching up to eat. We also leave tree stumps, so the rhinos can rub their hides, other animals can satisfy territorial instincts by scenting with urine, and deer can rub the velvet off their antlers. Then there are animals like the sitatunga (the most aquatic of antelopes), which need places to go where they can get away from the other species. They like to hide along the stream that runs through the East Africa exhibit, and also down around the lake at the lower end of the exhibit."

While some visitors said they would prefer to see the Park's hills and valleys covered with grass, it was important to the staff to meet the animals' needs. Killmar explained that "We have to leave certain areas in their dry, natural state so that animals that dislike grass or wet areas can still retreat to where they won't feel stressed. Also, mothers of certain species need suitably rough or rocky terrain to hide or 'tuck' their babies, an important anti-predator instinct. We'd also be negligent if we didn't consider the needs of animals like zebras, which groom themselves by rolling in dust."

With its height and long neck, the South African greater kudu *Tragelaphus strepsiceros strepsiceros* reaches up to browse.

Dr. Schroeder's drive and far-sightedness realized a dream that continues today.

All smiles: Dr. Schroeder and Society president Anderson Borthwick on opening day for the public, May 10, 1972.

A joint effort: Collaboration has been the key to bringing the California condor *Gymnogyps californianus* back from the brink.

For Today and Tomorrow

The Park has had success breeding the highly endangered Somali wild ass *Equus africanus somalicus*.

Since its founding, the San Diego Wild Animal Park has joined the San Diego Zoo to play an indispensable role in the worldwide efforts by zoologists and conservationists to save as many wild animal species as possible from extinction. Today, the Wild Animal Park is a busy, lush, and breathtakingly beautiful setting for its important conservation and education work. As Charles Bieler, executive director emeritus of the Society, commented on the tenth anniversary of the Park in 1982, "Ongoing efforts here are essential if we are to provide an opportunity for our children and grandchildren to see many of the wonderful creatures that are dwindling in their native habitats and that soon may not be available ever again for viewing in the wild." ✵ At this printing, the Wild Animal Park is home to about 3,600 animals comprising 418 species and subspecies, including 56 endangered species. Captive breeding efforts have been and continue to be highly successful, and the survival rate for newborns is more than 80 percent, estimated to be five times higher than in the wild.

This remarkable success in propagating such a diverse cast of characters is a tribute to the Wild Animal Park's increasingly sophisticated management techniques, experience, and collaborative efforts by curators, keepers, veterinarians, and researchers. Considerable attention is given to the endangered and threatened species living at the Wild Animal Park, but the staff knows that their success with all the resident species can have long-range implications. Conditions in the wild can change swiftly, and species that appear "stable" can suddenly go into decline, given the effects of deforestation, drought, human warfare, poaching, or the inexorable crush of human population demands. ✵ Dr. Dolan has summed up the Park staff's strong, ongoing sense of purpose in saying, "We believe that places like the Wild Animal Park, working together with other zoos, offer the best hope of safeguarding the incredible diversity of the world's wildlife species."

Hope for the future: One of the Wild Animal Park's main goals is to conserve endangered species, like these Sumatran tigers *Panthera tigris sumatrae.*

Join Us on an Incredible Journey

A visit to the San Diego Wild Animal Park is like magically stepping from the hustle and bustle of Southern California into the mysteries of exotic, far-away lands. Leave your cares behind as you enter the Park's thatched portal, designed after the ceremonial chamber of a Ugandan king, and set foot upon the path to adventure. Your first encounter is with the thatched huts, open-air markets, and wooden pathways of **Nairobi Village**. Here you will find amenities for humans, such as shops, restaurants, snacks, shady places to rest, areas for children to play and explore, and information. But there is also wildlife everywhere you turn in the Village, everything from birds to primates to small hoofed stock to insects. Enjoy your discovery of the wonders awaiting you here.

Playtime paradise.

Whether you're strolling along admiring the view or scampering from one fun place to another, Nairobi Village has something for everyone.

The trickster.

The black heron *Egretta ardesiaca* of central and southern Africa has a sneaky but very effective way of catching its aquatic prey. It raises its wings above its head, dipping the wingtips down to form an umbrella, then leans forward to cast a shadow on the surface of the water. Fish are fooled into thinking this is a safe shady spot and swim into the shadows— only to be snatched up as dinner.

Golden-breasted starling *Cosmopsarus regius magnificus*

It pays to be flexible.

The bald ibis *Geronticus calvus* lives in marshes and wetlands in southern Africa, where many of the original forests have disappeared and there are few large trees for nesting. Instead, this adaptable species nests on sandstone cliffs, often beside waterfalls that are inaccessible to predators.

European roller *Coracias garrulus garrulus*

Avian Africa

You'll know you've left the city behind as you enter the lush, green environs of the walk-through **African Aviary**. Exotic calls greet you as you glimpse flashes of color overhead and in the trees, and identification keys help you find the many and varied feathered inhabitants. 🐾 The birds are native to the areas of Africa with lakes and streams, where they find their food of fish, frogs, snails, and aquatic plants. Some, however, can be found on the open savannas, perching on the few trees to wait for insects to eat. Spend some time in the African Aviary and you will discover an amazing assortment of behaviors that reveal the nature and adaptations of these avian wonders: nest-building, territorial displays, courtship, preening, and feeding, among others.

Escargot, anyone?

The African open-bill stork *Anastomus lamelligerus lamelligerus* **gets its common name from the seemingly odd shape of its bill: both the upper and lower parts curve to form an open "hole" in the center. This oddity is actually quite useful in catching and eating the stork's main food—snails. The Wild Animal Park was the first captive facility in the world to successfully breed this unusual species.**

Flying underwater.

The African darter *Anhinga rufa rufa*, **also called the snake bird, swims for its supper by diving underwater and using its wings and webbed feet to chase fish. Its legs and feet, which are placed far back on the body, make walking awkward but make great propellers. Cormorants and darters lack any oils or waterproofing agents in their feathers, which helps them swim better, but the feathers become waterlogged. When they emerge they become sun worshippers, spreading their wings out to dry.**

The lily-trotter.

The African jacana *Actophilornis africana* has the singular ability to walk on water—or at least that's what it looks like. It has extremely long toes that distribute its weight and give it such good balance that it can run along the surface of ponds by stepping on lily pads and other floating vegetation.

Duck, duck, ...goose?

One of the smallest waterfowl species, the African pygmy goose *Nettapus auritus* is not really a goose at all. It is a duck species that belongs to the group known as perching ducks, named for their ability to perch on branches unlike most other waterfowl. It nests in decayed cavities of trees, and its ducklings have sharp claws and stiff tails to aid them in climbing out of the holes after they hatch.

A day at the shore.

The long-toed lapwing *Vanellus crassirostris* is one of the plovers and lives along the shores of African lakes and marshes. Long-legged as well as long-toed for mucking about in muddy or sandy soil, this quick bird uses its large eyes to locate prey such as insects, then uses a "run-and-snatch" technique to capture it. The WIld Animal Park was the first facility in the world to breed this species in captivity.

White-bellied bustard
Eupodotis senegalensis

High roller.

The blue-bellied roller *Coracias cyanogaster* gets its common name from the spectacular twisting or rolling motions it makes high in the air during courtship and territorial flights. Raucous calls, brightly colored plumage, and swift dives to the ground to capture large insects or small animals make roller species a conspicuous part of the African landscape.

Lounging at the Lagoon

Great blue heron *Ardea herodias*

At the heart of Nairobi Village is **Mombasa Lagoon**, surrounded by paths, wooden walkways, and a simulation of a Congo fishing village. This peaceful watering hole is home to pelicans, storks, flamingos, and ducks, along with the many migratory bird visitors, like herons (left) and egrets, that are not part of the Wild Animal Park's collection but make use of the Park's hospitality each year. Reeds, grasses, lilies, and other water-loving plants thrive along the edges of the lagoon, creating a lovely picture for visitors who find a bench and sit for awhile. Local hummingbirds hover around the brightly colored blossoms of flowering vines, and coral trees add their exotic beauty to the view. ❧ Outside the lagoon, exhibits are scattered around one corner and the next, for primates such as spider monkeys and Gabriella's crested gibbons, hoofed stock such as babirusas and dik-diks, and small carnivores such as meerkats. These exhibits provide close encounters with some of the Park's intriguing smaller species.

Living large.

In terms of body weight, pink-backed pelicans *Pelecanus rufescens*, along with the other pelican species, are among the largest of all flying birds. The most conspicuous part of a pelican is its huge bill and expandable gular pouch, which can hold three times the amount of fish that the bird's stomach can. Pink-backed pelicans live in large colonies and nest in trees. They feed by scooping fish out of the water as they swim, and several pelicans may work together to herd fish into shallow waters for easy picking.

Good things come to those who wait.

The shoebill *Balaeniceps rex* may be the most patient bird in the world—it is often mistaken for a statue as it stands perfectly still, waiting for an unsuspecting fish to glide by. But once they spy one, these large birds lunge into action so swiftly that their prey is unlikely to escape. These comical-looking storks get their common name from the scientist who described them— he felt that the storks' bills looked like the clogs worn as shoes.

High wire acrobats.

Fearlessly negotiating small branches high in the rain forest canopy, Colombian brown spider monkeys *Ateles belzebuth hybridus* can outdo any circus daredevil. To help them accomplish these feats, they have exceptionally long arms and legs in proportion to their bodies, and a prehensile tail that they use as a fifth arm or leg. In fact, the tail is so flexible and strong that a spider monkey can hang from it alone and can even pick up objects with it. These South American primates live in groups of up to 30 individuals and maintain distinct territories. They feed mostly on fruit, although they won't turn down nuts, flowers, insects, and bird eggs as they forage.

Chattering masked bandits.

Few sights are more animated than a group of ring-tailed lemurs *Lemur catta* running, tumbling, leaping, and climbing. Their most conspicuous feature is the long, fluffy, black-and-white ringed tail, which they use as a signal to one another and as a comfy blanket to keep warm while they sleep. They are extremely curious and sometimes even sneaky, stealing food from one another when the occasion arises. Like other lemurs, they are also sun worshippers, lifting their chins and spreading their arms to bask blissfully in the warmth.

Red alert.

As you stroll around Nairobi Village, look for various species of coral trees *Erythrina* sp. with their startling bright-red flowers. Some of these trees bloom when they don't have any leaves, a visual surprise you'll particularly notice in January. Coral trees are a widely varied bunch: some have medicinal properties, some are planted as shade trees on coffee and cocoa plantations, some have flowers that can be cooked and eaten, and some are poisonous.

Diminutive and delicate.

Cavendish's dik-dik *Madoqua kirkii cavendishi* is one of the tiniest antelope species, measuring about 14 inches at the shoulder and weighing only about 10 pounds. What they may lack in body size, however, is made up by their acute senses: they have extremely large eyes and ears, and an elongated, almost proboscis-like nose, all of which they use to assess their surroundings and be on the alert for predators. They live alone, in pairs, or rarely in small groups, and mark their territory by rubbing against sticks and grasses with the glands found at the base of their eyes.

Alien swine.

If the Vulcans on *Star Trek* had pigs, this is what they would look like. There's speculation that the large, pointed ears of the red river hog *Potamochoerus porcus* may be used in territorial or dominance displays, but they certainly look amusing. These forest-dwelling pigs are native to Africa, where they use their sensitive yet tough snouts to root up tubers, roots, insects, and worms. In fact, rooting is their speciality—at the Wild Animal Park they make short work of their exhibit, including digging up large boulders with ease on a regular basis.

Salt of the earth.

The Andes might seem like an odd place to find flamingos, but for many Chilean flamingos *Phoenicopterus chilensis*, these high mountains are home. They live 13,000 feet above sea level, on lakes that are more salty than the ocean, and they often create the characteristic flamingo nests on mounds of salt crystals formed by evaporation of the lake water. They also feed in this harsh environment—they sift algae, brine shrimp, and worms out of the mud and silt by using their specialized, sieve-like bills.

Sparring with spurs.

When two spurred tortoises *Geochelone sulcata* get into a fight, they attack with an unusual weapon: their hind legs. That's where the sharp, horny projections called spurs are, and they jab at one another with them. People sometimes think that the spurs are used for digging, because these tortoises dig out underground burrows by using their hind legs, as well. But their feet are the real shovels in those excavations. Spurred tortoises are native to arid regions of central Africa, and they can survive extended periods of drought by remaining in their burrows and entering a state of torpor.

A duck by any other name might be a teal.

The falcated teal *Anas falcata* (below) and the Cape teal *Anas capensis*, among others, are ducks known as "dabblers." That's because they dabble at the water's surface, feeding on aquatic plants, insects, small fish, and crustaceans like shrimp. During the breeding season, usually from spring to early summer, the males of these species can be readily spotted by their brightly colored, iridescent plumage, which they use to attract females.

The littlest deer.

The southern pudu *Pudu puda* lives in the tropical forests of Chile and Argentina, where it is a master of escape and evasion. This one-foot-tall deer's low-slung body, sturdy legs, and nimble hooves allow it to be fleet of foot among rocks and even along the tops of fallen tree trunks, and when pursued it runs in a zig-zag pattern to confuse its attacker.

Prickly plants.

Animals aren't the only ones that defend themselves against a threat—plants also have some very effective deterrents. Acacias grow impressive thorns, four inches long in some species, designed to make a hungry herbivore think twice about feasting on the leaves. This trick doesn't work very well with giraffes, however. With their long, tough tongues, they just work around the thorns! Acacias are one of the Zoological Society's main plant collections, and you'll see many types as you explore the Wild Animal Park. Look for the paperbark *Acacia sieberiana* var. *woodii*, with its peeling, papery bark, and the fever tree *Acacia xanthophloea* (above), so named because it's native to swampy areas of Africa where malaria is also found. But that's just a coincidence—the trees don't carry malaria, mosquitoes do.

Fearless scorpion eater.

Suricates *Suricata suricatta*, commonly known as meerkats, are highly social members of the same family as mongooses, and they build extensive underground burrow systems to house their colonies. When babies are born, the entire colony looks out for them, and one adult is always left to babysit the youngsters while the rest go out on hunting parties for food. They gobble up things like insects and worms as they go, and they work collectively to tackle larger prey or to defend against an enemy. One of their favorite foods is a juicy scorpion—the meerkats are so quick at biting that they rarely get stung. But even if they do, they seem to be immune to the scorpion's venom.

A tusked wonder.

The first thing you may notice about the male Sulawesi babirusa *Babyrousa babyrussa celebensis* is that it has tusks growing on the top of its snout. So how did its teeth end up on its nose? The upper canines, which are continually growing and elongated into tusks, actually grow up into the babirusa's soft palate and end up breaking the skin to emerge on the nose. These are complimented by the lower canines, also tusks, that curve upward and are honed on trees to become quite sharp. Both are used by the males for fighting and may be used for rooting, as well. These unusual tusks also give this swine species its name—the Sulawesi natives say the tusks look like the antlers of a deer, and babirusa means "pig deer."

"It don't mean a thing if you ain't got that swing."

You'd be hard put to find a primate that could swing through the trees faster and with more agility than a Gabriella's crested gibbon *Hylobates gabriellae*. *Hylobates* means "dweller in the trees," and these primates more than live up to the name, with their superior agility and rapid movement through the forest. They travel by swinging from branch to branch, often with such long swings that they look like they are flying. Gibbons are also famous for their loud, resonate calls, often a duet between a female and her mate, which declare their territory and their intention to defend it.

Romping with rhinos.

One of the Animal Care Center's responsibilities is to care for young animals that have injuries or are not being cared for by their mothers. This has included several rhinos over the years, including Jomo (left), an East African black rhinoceros *Diceros bicornis michaeli* **that arrived at the ACC on his birthday, July 22, 1995. The keepers had noticed that the newborn had trouble standing and following his mother, and it turned out he had weak and curved legs. His bones had not yet set, so the veterinarians put casts on his legs to straighten them. He only wore the casts for a few days, then gained strength by exercising. And his favorite exercise was to push at the keepers with his head then run around his corral—in fact, he liked this so much that he whined for more when the keepers had to leave to get their work done!**

Ah, Youth!

Radar the fennec fox
Vulpes zerda **was raised at the Animal Care Center.**

One of Nairobi Village's treats is a visit to the **Animal Care Center** (ACC), which houses adorable baby animals that need to be hand raised. Seen through viewing windows, these youngsters have most often been rejected by their mothers for some reason, or they may have been sick or injured and require human help as they recover. A wide variety of species may need the Care Center's services, anything from hoofed stock like antelope, deer, and rhinos to primates like bonobos and gorillas. ❧ The Park's veterinarians and the Care Center keepers use their specialized skills to determine the best formulas, diets, physical exercises, and social care for each baby that comes through the door, and round-the-clock care can be provided for baby animals in jeopardy. Of course, the ideal goal is to have as few babies here as possible, indicating that their mothers are providing good maternal care. But even without babies, the Animal Care Center has interesting surprises, like the tamandua family that lives permanently in one of the exhibit areas. ❧ And just next door, kids and kids at heart will find the **Petting Kraal**, where visitors can mingle with tolerant, easy-going species of goats, sheep, antelopes, and deer.

Lion kings.

When their mother became ill and could not care for them, Maji and Mashoni, two male Transvaal lions *Panthera leo krugeri*, took up residence at the Animal Care Center. They were born in the field exhibit on August 1, 1995, and had been with mom for two weeks before they were found cold and hungry. Once they were stabilized, the cubs immediately began winning friends and admirers by wrestling, chasing, stalking, and pouncing on one another, much like domestic kittens. The keepers had the envious job of feeding the cubs their formula and occasionally joining in the rough-and-tumble play. The cubs demonstrated typical lion behaviors as they grew, like dragging towels around as if they were prey and greeting the keepers with the characteristic "head bonk." One thing about them was less than fierce, however: Their favorite companion, next to the keepers, was a duck—a large plush toy duck that they loved to sleep with.

Foul play.

In its South American rain forest home, the Guianan tamandua *Tamandua tetradactyla tetradactyla*, or lesser anteater, is called *caguare* by the local people—which translates to "forest stinker." This does not refer to a bad disposition, although tamanduas can inflict serious injuries with their long, sharp claws when threatened, but rather to their particular odor, produced by glandular secretions. Smelling foul is a means of defense, often sending predators running in the other direction. The Animal Care Center has its own resident family of tamanduas, which, with their prehensile tails and arboreal nature, are usually perched, folded, and wrapped around their climbing structure. In the wild tamanduas eat ants and termites with their long, sticky tongues, so the keepers create a special gruel for the Park's residents, made of dry cat food and primate biscuits ground to a paste with water.

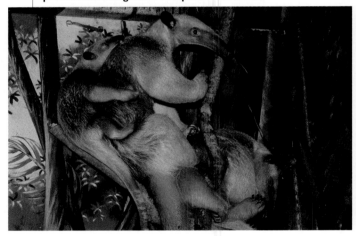

Keeper Marcia Diehl feeds a greedy zebra foal.

Bouncing baby bonobo.

Among the great apes, raising offspring is a big responsibility, and on occasion a young and inexperienced mother, particularly one that hasn't observed maternal care within her troop, doesn't know what to do when she gives birth. Neglect becomes a serious problem for the newborn very quickly, and sometimes the keepers have to intervene. This was the case for Ikela, a bonobo *Pan paniscus*, who was born on November 27, 1991. She became the center of attention at the Animal Care Center, and required regular feedings, being held, exercise to strengthen her muscles, and a great deal of interaction to teach her the rules of being a bonobo. She apparently learned her lessons well, because she is now a well-adjusted adult.

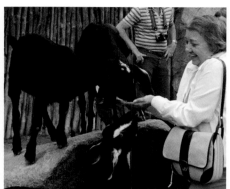

Reach out and touch someone.

The urge to touch is irresistible, and the Petting Kraal offers a very satisfactory tactile experience. A good-natured bunch of sheep and goats—some domestic, some exotic—are waiting to say hello, along with perhaps some deer, antelopes, or even pigs.

Brilliant, mate!

Brightly and boldly colored green-nape lorikeets
Trichoglossus haematodus haematodus **are found
in New Guinea. These small parrots are very
social, foraging in parties of up to 50 birds and
roosting at night in groups that may number in
the thousands. It's common to see them hanging out in human areas—their cousins in
Australia regularly frequent people's backyards.**

A Rainbow on Your Shoulder

Down the path from the Animal Care Center is the bustle and chatter
of **Lorikeet Landing**. There, you'll find that things are hopping as you enter an aviary
designed for personal encounters with dozens of green-nape lorikeets, which fly among
visitors and perch on arms, shoulders, and even heads. Green-nape lorikeets are active,
intelligent, and curious little parrots native to New Guinea that look as if they have
been painted in vivid shades of blue, red, yellow, and green. Lorikeets are nectar feed-
ers, and visitors may purchase small cups of a nectar solution to offer the eager flock.
No one's allowed to be shy in this exhibit—if you hang back in a corner, be assured
the birds will come to you to see if you're holding out on the nectar supply!

It's on the tip of their tongues.

The brush they use to feed with, that is. Lories and lorikeets have a unique adaptation that allows them to extract the pollen and nectar they eat from flowers—a specialized tongue with elongated papillae on the sides and tip that bend inward to form a kind of brush. The birds also eat fruit, berries, and leaf buds, and when they eat these more solid foods, the brush-like papillae are enclosed in a special sheath for protection.

You can't help but smile.

For photographers, Lorikeet Landing provides a wealth of photo opportunities. Whether it's a wide-eyed child with several birds perched on his arm, three old friends beaming broadly with a dozen lorikeets all around them, or your usually stoic uncle laughing while lorikeets adorn his hat and demand his attention, this interactive exhibit is bound to delight one and all and produce some extraordinary memories for the photo album.

Orange flame butterfly *Dryas julia*

Blue morpho butterfly *Morpho peleides*

Butterflies flutter by.

There are many different species of butterflies to discover in Hidden Jungle, some large and exotic, like the owl butterfly, the blue morpho, and the clear-wing butterfly, others small and stunning, like the orange flame, the zebra-striped, and the delicate tree nymph. But they all started out the same way—as caterpillars, some fuzzy, some spiny, and some spotted. Once these caterpillars have munched their way through enough leaves to store up energy, they then begin the process of metamorphosis by encasing themselves in a cocoon and becoming pupae. This is the stage in which they arrive at the Wild Animal Park, some smooth and rounded, others looking like curled, dead leaves. Hidden Jungle has its own "cocoon room," where the pupae are carefully hung from styrofoam rods and kept at the appropriate temperature and humidity. When the butterflies emerge, they are given time to dry and test their wings, and when they are ready, they are released into the main part of the greenhouse exhibit to flutter and float among the plants.

White morpho butterfly *Morpho polyphemus*

The cocoon room: A keeper in Hidden Jungle carefully hangs pupae.

Life Among the Leaves

Birdwing butterfly
Ormithoptera priamus

We all pay attention to the impressive size of elephants and the playful antics of monkeys, but what about the tiny creatures, the ones that live their lives out almost unnoticed, hidden from view? **Hidden Jungle**, a glass-walled greenhouse exhibit, spotlights this minute world and its fascinating activities. Here you will find rare and exotic butterfly species that seem to float instead of fly, shy forest birds with beautiful plumage, the fanciful acrobatics of hummingbirds, industrious and resourceful leaf-cutter ants, and—for those that don't have the phobia—arachnids like tarantulas and scorpions (enclosed, of course!). ❧ Filled with lush plantings and botanical beauties of the rain forest, Hidden Jungle will show you the delight and wonder of looking under and among the leaves, instead of just above them.

An ancient lineage.

Fossil images of staghorn ferns *Platycerium* sp. have been found that date back 500 million years, and they reveal that ferns were the first plants to evolve true leaves. Staghorn ferns are still plentiful today because they are hardy and adaptable. Although they occur most often in tropical regions, some species can withstand temperatures as low as 25 degrees Fahrenheit for short periods of time. Staghorn ferns are epiphytes, meaning that they grow on trees and other plants without harming them, and they obtain their nourishment from moisture in the air, rainfall, and dead fronds that gather in the center of the plant and form a kind of compost. Their appearance led to their scientific name: *Platycerium* derives from two Greek words meaning "broad horn," because the lower fronds resemble a stag's antlers.

On the march.

In a special exhibit within Hidden Jungle, you'll find a thoroughly interesting, and completely authorized, invasion of ants. But these aren't just any ants—they are leafcutter ants *Atta cephalotus*, those talented denizens of the rain forest floor that precisely and expertly cut pieces of leaves and carry them back to the nest. They measure the leaf sections with their legs, they cut them with their huge mandibles, and they carry them suspended over their heads on the trek back to the colony. Why go to so much trouble? Because leafcutter ants have a symbiotic relationship with an unlikely partner—fungus—that requires the leaves to grow on. In turn, the ants eat the nutritious, swollen tips that the fungus produces. Another interesting aspect of colony life is that all its members, whether worker, soldier, or attendant to the queen, are female—they are all sterile, and they are all sisters. The queen is the only ant that reproduces, and she only produces females until environmental conditions signal that it's time for some fertile males. They don't get to stick around, though—they fly away to meet up with receptive fertile female ants in a one-time mating ritual, and then the males die.

Western emerald hummingbird *Amazilia amazilia amazilia*

Colombian sparkling violet-ear *Colibri coruscans coruscans*

Glittering jewels.

Zooming, flitting, and hovering, their iridescent feathers reflecting the light in jewel tones of blue, green, and purple, hummingbirds are sure to capture your attention. They have captured the imaginations of people for centuries and have been the subject of many colorful myths and legends. The Mayans called the hummingbird *zumzum*, **for the sound the wings make, and the Aztecs called it** *Huitzili*, **which means "shining one with the weapon like a cactus thorn." At one time it was thought that hummingbirds never landed and had no feet, but of course they do and use them for perching to survey their territory. Despite their diminutive size, hummingbirds like the sparkling violet-ear** *Colibri coruscans* **and the emerald hummingbird** *Amazilia amazilia* **are aggressive and fearless, largely because few predators can catch them. In order to accomplish their rapid flight and hovering, helicopter-like motions, their wings move at about 50 to 70 beats per second, and during aerial maneuvers for courtship, this can be as high as 200 beats per second. Their hearts beat about 1,200 times per minute, and they must consume more than half their body weight each day in insects and nectar to maintain their extremely high metabolic rate. They have achieved the smallest body size possible for a warm-blooded animal, and their nests are about the size of half a walnut shell. One of their favorite materials for nest building is spider webs—so the keepers make sure there is a ready supply, along with animal fur and plant fibers.**

Cozy in my spider webs: An emerald hummingbird chick in its tiny nest.

A male emerald hummingbird at rest.

A world in a plant.

Bromeliads are a large group of rain forest plants that are quite at home in Hidden Jungle. Perhaps best known are the species with tightly overlapping leaves that direct moisture down toward the roots. As this moisture gathers, it creates a reservoir in the center of the plant, and the plant produces its blossoms just above the surface. This system provides the means of pollination: When insects or animals disturb the surface of the water, the blossoms dip and move and pollen is transferred from the anther to the pistil. These types of bromeliads can actually house entire ecosystems, with microorganisms that gather in the pooled water, which are eaten by insects and their larvae, which in turn feed salamanders, snails, and frogs.

Hey, that branch is walking!

An adult female giant wingless walkingstick *Pharnacia acanthopus* can reach 10 inches in length, and because it resembles a tree branch in almost every way, you may only notice it when it moves! Hidden Jungle has three species of stick insects, including the giant thorny stick insect *Heteropteryx dilatata*. The females of this species can reach lengths of up to nine inches, and they have leaf-shaped abdomens for camouflage. Their legs are also lined with sharp spines, and if the insect feels threatened she will draw her legs together repeatedly in a pinching motion—very uncomfortable for the object being pinched.

The Guianan white-bearded manakin *Manacus manacus manacus* gets its common name from puffing out its throat feathers during breeding displays.

Where's the bug? The wooden stick in this photo is in the middle; on top at the left is a nymph of the giant wingless walkingstick *Pharnacia acanthopus,* and hanging below is an adult female.

A viridescent female giant thorny stick insect *Heteropteryx dilatata.*

Hail to the emperor!

The impressive emperor scorpion *Pandinus imperator* in the Crevasse section of Hidden Jungle is among the largest scorpions in the world. It sports the well-known and formidable stinger on its tail, but it actually uses its large claws to catch and crush prey. The venomous stinger is used for defense or to subdue prey. Scorpion babies are born live, and they crawl up on to the mother's back and stay there until they molt—when they are big enough to not be eaten by their relatives.

Jeepers, creepers!

The **Surinam green honeycreeper** *Chlorophanes spiza spiza* **is one of a group of birds sometimes called flower-piercers, because they use their long, thin bills to probe flowers for nectar. They also eat fruit, and they hawk insects out of the air. These colorful little birds are monogamous, and the male feeds and protects the female while she incubates the eggs.**

Don't call me an insect.

Despite the creepy crawly similarity, spiders, tarantulas, and scorpions aren't insects—they're arachnids. What's the difference? Well, arachnids have eight legs instead of six, two body parts instead of three, and they don't have antennae or wings. Tarantulas like this baboon spider *Theraphosa* sp. make silk like other spiders do, but they use it to line their underground burrows instead of making webs. Tarantulas also have the enviable ability to shed their skins and start anew. As they grow they molt, a process in which their outer carapace splits and separates until they can literally crawl out of it. The old skin remains almost completely intact and looks startlingly like a second spider.

Incubation duty.

Guianan turquoise tanager *Tangara mexicana mexicana*

Tropical hues.

Forest-dwelling tanagers are brilliantly colored, and most sport their bold finery year-round. They are mostly fruit-eaters, although they snap up insects and spiders as well while they forage, often plucking them from the undersides of leaves. They play a vital role in the distribution of tropical American trees and shrubs, because they don't digest the seeds they swallow and carry them to other parts of the forest in their droppings.

Bay-headed tanager *Tangara gyrola*

Western golden-masked tanager *Tangara larvata franciscae*

Jungle gems.

With their fanciful shapes and extraordinary colors and patterns, orchids have long been considered some of the most beautiful and exotic blossoms in the world. Orchids are one of the main plant collections maintained by the Zoological Society of San Diego, and Hidden Jungle provides the bright, warm, and moist environment in which they thrive. You'll find *Angraecums, Cattleyas, Cymbidiums, Phalaenopsis, Epidendrums, Dendrobiums,* and *Oncidiums,* among many other types of orchids, including some spectacular hybrids. Pay attention to the elaborate curls, flounces, lips, and colors of the flowers, all of which are designed to attract pollinators—orchids could hardly be accused of being subtle or shy!

Epidendrum prismatucarpum

Ascocenda hybrid

Cattleya granulosa

The Gentle Giants

Off the beaten path and tucked into a shady pocket of Nairobi Village, you'll discover the **Gorilla Habitat**, home to the Wild Animal Park's family of western lowland gorillas *Gorilla gorilla gorilla*. Winston, the adult male silverback, is the troop's gentle leader, a good-natured fellow by all accounts that has not only been tolerant of but also helpful in the reintroduction of hand-raised juveniles. If the other gorillas pick on the newcomer, Winston will intervene, and he has been observed sitting quietly next to the youngster in a comforting way. He is the boss, but two subordinate males await their chance to lead a troop some day, Paul Donn and Kubatiza. The adult females—Vila, Alberta, Camilla, Ione, and Penny—have all given birth to at least one offspring, and five of those youngsters—Mbili, Ndjia, Ndjole, Kebara, and Jamani—provide the ongoing ruckus and playtime in the exhibit. ❧ Although historically gorillas have had a reputation as fierce, ravaging beasts that attack without provocation, they are in fact one of the most gentle and peaceful primate species. They would rather slip quietly away from danger than confront it, although the males will display and charge to protect the troop if they feel threatened. But even that is often just a bluff—if the intruder goes away, a gorilla will not follow to make good on his threat.

Winston is the gorilla troop's current silverback—the dominant adult male and leader. He follows in the footsteps of the late Trib, who was much loved by keepers and visitors for his genial good nature and gentle way with the troop's little ones. Winston is living up to that reputation admirably, also showing an ease with his role as head of the family.

Vila is the granny of the group. She was born in 1957 and came to the Zoo at about one year of age. Vila has had two offspring of her own: Alvila, one of the adult female gorillas living in Gorilla Tropics at the Zoo, and Alberta, who lives with her mother at the Wild Animal Park. She is also the grand-mother of Ione and the great-grandmother of Jumani. As an elderly gorilla, she is helping the keepers and veterinarians learn more about primate geriatrics as they discover ways to improve her health, diet, and mobility.

Alberta made headlines when she adopted Kebara (right), an infant that Penny, a young and inexperienced mother, was not caring for. After giving birth, Penny was exhausted and bewildered, and would not hold Kebara, who was crying loudly. Alberta was in another room with her own 10-month-old baby, but she was clearly aware of Kebara's distress. She reached under the partly closed partition and began to pull the newborn slowly toward her, watching to see if Penny would intervene. When she didn't, Alberta picked Kebara up and began to nurse her—and Kebara became her adopted baby. In an interesting twist, her 10-month-old, Ndjole (left), then began to spend time with Penny. Because Penny was still producing milk, Ndjole began nursing from her—and Penny became her adopted mom. So in essence, the two mothers had swapped their children as the result of the circumstances. After about a year, the young gorillas then swapped back to their own birth mothers, and now Ndjole and Kebara have close ties to both of the adult females.

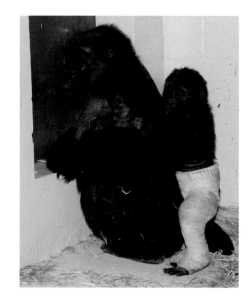

Ndjia was certainly a trooper in the troop when she overcame an injury that left her with a weak and short leg. No one was aware of it at the time, but somewhere during her first year, Ndjia had suffered a fracture to the thigh bone in her left leg that had damaged the growth plate. When she was a little over a year old, the keepers and veterinarians could see that the leg was not growing, and that it would probably atrophy and might have to be amputated. Specialists in human pediatric orthopedics were brought in from San Diego's Children's Hospital to perform surgery, and Ndjia spent one month in a hip-to-toe cast. Her mother, Kamilah, eagerly accepted Ndjia back after the surgery, cast and all, and Ndjia didn't let her immobilized leg stop her from playing. Once the cast was removed, there was a suspenseful six-month waiting period to see if the leg would begin to grow again—and it did. The surgery was a complete success, and Ndjia was soon giving piggy-back rides to her younger cousins.

Seeing red.

The northern carmine bee eater *Merops nubicus nubicus* is unusual among bee eaters because of its coloring, which is largely red and blue instead of green. But like the other species, it is graceful, agile, and dextrous in its swift and sure capture of bees.

A cozy burrow—for a bird?

Have you ever seen a bird dig out an underground burrow? Well, you might at the Bee Eater Aviary, because all bee eaters, including this white-throated bee eater *Merops albicollis*, dig holes into the banks of rivers or into sandy ground that they use as nests. Their nesting colonies can sometimes reach a thousand or more holes.

Bees Beware

Near the gorillas, you'll chance upon an aviary of truly remarkable birds with some specialized skills, the **Bee Eater Aviary**. Bee eaters do indeed eat bees, as well as wasps, ants, and butterflies, which they catch in mid-air by diving swiftly and gracefully from a high perch. They are specialists in eating stinging insects and have developed a fascinating technique for removing the toxic threat. With a wriggling bee in its narrow, pointed beak, a bee eater seeks a perch of suitable branches. It then strikes the insect repeatedly against the perch to kill it, and rubs the bee against the branch to expel the sting and the venom. Expertly prepared in this manner, the insect becomes a perfect meal. The Park's aviary invites visitors to witness this interesting behavior, as well as marvel at the bright colors of bee eater species.

Blue streak.

The seasonal migration of the western blue-cheeked bee eater *Merops superciliosus chrysocercus* is a spectacular sight, as large numbers of these colorful birds travel well-established routes between northern and western Africa.

All in the family.

Bee eaters, like this common white-fronted bee eater *Merops bullockoides bullockoides*, have an interesting social structure that includes "helpers," which are juvenile or non-breeding birds in the colony that help the breeding pairs raise their chicks. These helpers are usually related to the chicks, often as older siblings or "cousins." The advantage is that more chicks are raised successfully this way, and the helpers learn what they need to know to raise their own chicks some day.

Lolita, a double-yellow headed parrot, sings for her audience.

Clarence the cinereous vulture may be clumsy, but he gets the job done!

On Stage

Do opposums really play dead? Come and find out at the Rare and Wild America Show!

The Wild Animal Park's animal residents are all entertaining in their own unique ways, but we also have some stage performers that love to be in the spotlight. ❧ At the Benbough Amphitheater, you can cheer on an amazing array of feathered friends in the exciting and interactive **Bird Show**. These avian artists will have you oo-ing and ah-ing, clapping and laughing as they demonstrate their talented behaviors. ❧ At the Village Amphitheater, you can experience **Rare and Wild America** as some familiar and not-so-familiar critters show you what they can do. Whether it's the sleek grace of a mountain lion, the trundling antics of a porcupine, or the wise stare of a great horned owl, you'll discover a new-found appreciation for the animals that call America home. ❧ And near the Elephant Overlook, stop by for an **Elephant Encounter** that will show you how the keepers care for their large charges—and just how intelligent the ponderous pachyderms are!

Emus like Maxwell aren't known for intellectual prowess, but he eagerly does his part.

In this free-flight bird show, you may be the perch!

They look soft and fluffy, but North American porcupines have sharp barbs like their African cousins.

Sniffing out fame: This coatimundi has a nose for celebrity.

One of the elephant trainers explains how flexible and sensitive an elephant's trunk is.

All Aboard!

After an exploration of the sights and sounds in and around Nairobi Village, it's time for a safari into the Wild Animal Park's field exhibits, which represent geographical areas and habitats of Africa and Asia. Your **Wgasa Bush Line Railway Tour** departs from the railway boarding station near ThornTree Terrace in the Village, then glides quietly past those impressive pachyderms, the Asian and African elephants, sleek and sly Sumatran tigers and African lions, and beautiful but recalcitrant Grevy's zebras on its way into the main field exhibits. The open-sided trains provide you with a clear view of the Park's amazing vistas and its remarkable inhabitants. ❧ In this adventure, you are enclosed while the animals roam at their leisure through fields, hills, and valleys. Your guide will point out and name species as they come into view, then provide you with information on their native habitat, physical characteristics, eating habits, social behavior, and many other fascinating details. This 55-minute, guided excursion is different each time you take it, because even the narrators aren't sure what sights you might see around each curve. The animals have room to behave naturally, and that makes for some interesting spontaneity.

African bush elephant
Loxodonta africana africana

Wise matriarchs.

In the wild, elephants live in matriarchal herds of 6 to 50 related females, with one leader that is usually the oldest. The leader reinforces the herd's hierarchy, teaches the younger elephants social skills and survival techniques—such as where to find water during a drought—and uses her lifelong store of knowledge to choose foraging sites and avoid predators. The males live separately in what are known as "bachelor herds," except during the breeding season, when they are allowed to join the female herd for a few days. How do they know when they can approach? Elephants have a widely varied and complex communication system, and they make low frequency calls inaudible to humans that other elephants can hear from a mile away. There are only two species of elephants: Asian and African. The trick in knowing which is which is to remember that African elephants have the large ears shaped like the continent of Africa, and the Indian elephants have small ears and a rounded dome on their heads. The Wild Animal Park cares for small herds of both species, housed in separate enclosures that are each about two acres in size.

Asiatic elephants *Elephas maximus indicus*

"Tiger, tiger, burning bright…"

Upon encountering the majestic Sumatran tiger *Panthera tigris sumatrae*, it is clear what inspired William Blake's famous poem. The rich red-gold of the fur, the bold stripes, and that powerful, mesmerizing gaze make the tiger one of the world's most revered animals. It's a reverence that's mixed with a bit of fear, an appropriate reaction to a 250-pound, well-muscled, swift hunter with 1-inch-long claws and 3-inch-long canines. Unfortunately, the human fascination with these big cats has brought them to the brink of extinction. They have been hunted for their coats and for their body parts, which are used in some medicinal practices. Worldwide conservation measures to save the tiger include captive breeding efforts like those at the Wild Animal Park. Concentrating on the Sumatran tiger, the Park has had 15 cubs born.

It's good to be the king,

especially when the females do all the hard work of catching dinner. In the pride structure of the African Transvaal lion *Panthera leo krugeri*, the permanent social unit is the group of related females, which often spans several generations. These females live and hunt cooperatively, which enables lions to feed on large prey that other solitary cats could not kill by themselves. The lionesses procure the meal for the entire pride, but although the male only occasionally participates in a hunt, he always eats first. So does the king have any chores? His responsibilities are to challenge and run off any intruding lions, to father cubs, and to vigorously maintain the territorial boundaries. That's where the well-known lion roar comes in, which can be heard from a distance of four to five miles.

An equid with attitude.

Zebras are aggressive and defensive, and they are quick to respond to any threat. Yet they are also highly social, banding together in groups that can reach numbers of more than 100. How do cantankerous individuals live together in harmony? Zebras have worked it out by grooming one another. By using their large teeth, they pull out clumps of shedding hair, scratch one another, and remove parasites. This behavior has also led to a ritualized, bared-teeth grimace that is a greeting among zebras and neutralizes aggression. The Grevy's zebra *Equus grevyi* is the largest of the wild horse species and can be distinguished from the other zebra species by its narrow stripes. Grevy's zebras also have a different social structure: instead of living in established herds, they form loose associations based on the availability of food and mates.

Scratch my back, I'll scratch yours: Two Hartmann's mountain zebras demonstrate mutual grooming.

Energy-efficient pacifists.

Arabian oryxes *Oryx leucoryx* cope with their inhospitable environment in the deserts of central Arabia by being extremely tolerant of one another. In dry heat that can reach 122 degrees Fahrenheit, it does not pay to expend energy by fighting and competing. Instead, oryxes share what little shade is available under acacia trees and dig out shallow depressions in order to lie in the cooler sand. Aggressive encounters are few, except for challenging lone animals that try to join the herd. But even these animals are gradually accepted, as long as they play by the rules. The impressive horns found on both sexes can be used to defend a food source, if necessary, but such tussles are rare. The Arabian oryx is one of the Wild Animal Park's most celebrated success stories. The species had become extinct in the wild in 1972, but the Park had been participating in Operation Oryx and maintained a large portion of what was known as the World Herd. The captive breeding efforts of the San Diego Wild Animal Park, the Phoenix Zoo, and many other organizations went so well that it was possible to reintroduce small herds of Arabian oryxes to their native range in 1982, 1983, and 1990.

Mystic Hills

The first field exhibits you'll pass on your railway tour are the rocky and remote **Hillside Exhibits** on your left. These individual enclosures were designed for some of the animals that don't mix well with others, either because they are aggressive or shy. Look here for equine species like the eastern kiang and the highly endangered Somali wild ass. ❧ And you may even spy a unicorn—no, on closer inspection, it's an Arabian oryx, standing sideways so that its two slender horns look like one. There is speculation that the oryx might be the origin of the unicorn legends, and when you see this antelope species from afar, you can see why.

A tenacious spirit.

On the Tibetan plateau, which is sometimes called the "roof of the world," lives a hardy equine species called the eastern kiang *Equus kiang holdereri*, which ekes out a living and thrives where most animals could not. In an arid environment where vegetation only grows two to three months out of the year, this largest species of the wild asses must take advantage of the growing season to put on fat to last through the cold winter. This means eating even the tough, acid swamp grass that would lacerate the mouths of any other equids. Kiangs have hard, thick lips and a bony palate that make it possible for them to live on this daunting diet. The kiang herd at the Wild Animal Park has its own enclosure because the kiang's personality is in keeping with its survival instincts—it is a stubborn, spirited, and aggressive animal that insists upon dominating everything around it.

Survivors in the sand.

The land of the Somali wild ass *Equus africanus somalicus* is flat, arid, and stony, with hillocks that the animals stand on to scan the horizon. Temperatures soar as high as 122 degrees Fahrenheit during the day, and shade is scarce. Small herds of Somali wild asses are known to travel great distances after dark in search of waterholes, and they can last two to three days without drinking at all. These tough yet beautiful animals are a living part of Africa's history and are depicted in cave paintings in North Africa. At one time, sultans ordered a man's hand cut off if he killed a wild ass. However, this protection lapsed and the equids were killed for their skins and meat. Today, the Somali wild ass is critically endangered in the wild and is protected by the governments of Somalia and Ethiopia. The Wild Animal Park is involved in the captive breeding effort to save this species, and at this printing, eight Somali wild asses have been born at the Park.

Armor-plated tank.

At more than 4,000 pounds with thick, folded skin that looks like riveted plates, the male greater Indian rhinoceros *Rhinoceros unicornis* **is truly an awe-inspiring sight. Yet in spite of their imposing appearance, Indian rhinos, like other rhinos, have sensitive skin that is susceptible to sunburn and insect bites. That's why you'll often find a rhino wallowing at a waterhole, as it creates its own mud mask for protection. Indian rhinos have a hooked upper lip that can move almost like a finger, which places them in the group of browsing rhinos that feed on brush and small trees. They also have only one horn, which is what** *unicornis* **means. As with other rhinos, that horn has nearly been the downfall of the species—rhinos have been hunted almost to extinction for their horns, which are prized as magic talismans and powerful medicines in some cultures. Ironically, the people that use them might as well chew their own fingernails or hair instead of rhino horn—it's merely made up of the same keratin strands as human hair, matted into a compact shape for hardness.**

Passage to Asia

As the Wgasa Bush Line Railway moves up the valley, you enter the 60-acre **Asian Plains**, where Indian rhinoceroses wander by looking like welded and riveted tanks, several Asian deer species sport majestic antlers during the breeding season, and large antelope species graze in their established territories. It is interesting to note the distances between different groups, a natural buffer zone that develops just as it might in the wild. ❧ The species in this exhibit are varied and may come from quite different parts of Asia, yet each group has found its niche. And with no predators and less ongoing competition between males than in the wild, the environment is a fairly stable and harmonious one.

Semper paratus.

Like the Coast Guard and the Boy Scouts, the axis deer *Axis axis axis* is always prepared. Alert and watchful, it regularly raises its head while grazing to survey its surroundings. All deer have excellent senses, and they are most likely to first notice a threat by sound or smell. Catching sight of movement sends them bounding into the woods, tails raised like a white flag to warn other deer. Native to woodlands in India, the axis deer retains its spotted coat all its life, which helps it blend into dappled sunlight.

What in the world is a wapiti?

The wapiti is the largest member of the group known as red deer. Wapiti is the name Shawnee Indians gave these deer in North America, and because of similarity in size and appearance, the common name spread to seven different subspecies of red deer that live in habitats all over the world. And as if that weren't confusing enough, the wapiti is also sometimes called an elk. That's because European colonists thought these deer in the New World looked like the European elk—which is referred to over here as a moose! The Altai wapiti *Cervus elaphus sibiricus* at the Wild Animal Park hail from Siberia, where males and females form separate herds that can contain as many as 100 individuals.

A blackbuck sparring match.

Jumping blackbucks!

When one member in a herd of blackbucks *Antilope cervicapra* is alarmed, it jumps surprisingly high to warn the others. Then they all join in, each animal bounding into the air for several strides until the herd settles into a gallop to escape the danger. Considering that blackbucks can run at almost 50 miles per hour, few predators can keep up with them. This Indian antelope is one of the few species with different coloring for the males and females—the females are a consistent light brown, while the males have rich, black backs and sides in contrast to their white undersides.

The song of the gaur.

Judging from its appearance, the Indian gaur *Bos gaurus gaurus* may not seem particularly melodious, but the mating call of the males is reported to be a pleasant song of resonant notes that become successively lower. However, according to the keepers at the Wild Animal Park, you don't want to be to close to a singing gaur—these bovids are famous for having the worst breath of all the hoofed stock! Indian gaur live in forested hills and grassy clearings, grazing on grass and browsing on leaves. They are an endangered species, with only about 1,000 remaining in the wild, and the Wild Animal Park's herd is part of the captive breeding effort to save the species.

Swamp thing.

The barasingha *Cervus duvauceli duvauceli* lives in the marshy grasslands along the border of India and Nepal, which is the origin of its other common name—the swamp deer. It has unusually wide and elongated hooves as an adaptation for walking in water and mud. At one time, scientists believe these deer were plentiful in the open floodplains of the river systems in northern India. Today, however, these graceful animals are an endangered species because of extensive loss of their grassland habitat. Because female barasinghas breed just once a year in the wild, they do not reproduce as quickly as some species, further reducing their population numbers. At this printing, the San Diego Wild Animal Park maintains a herd of 24 barasinghas, and 291 have been born there, adding significantly to the world's population.

Sign language.

Like all gazelles, Persian goitered gazelles *Gazella subgutturosa subgutturosa* use an elaborate system of signs and signals to communicate, especially among the males. The head tilted back with the chin in the air is a warning; the head lowered slightly to point the horns outward is a threat; and the head down towards the ground with the horns pointing straight at the opponent is a direct challenge to fight. Males also scent mark to define their territories. They deposit feces in the same locations along the boundaries, and they leave secretions from glands below their eyes and in their ears on tall grass and brush. Why the name goitered gazelle? The males of this species have an enlarged larynx, which creates a bulge in the throat.

Mowing the fields of Africa.

Many animals keep Africa's savannas well groomed, but the southern white rhinoceros *Ceratotherium simum simum* is one of the most noticeable. It is a grazer, unlike its cousins the Indian and black rhinos, which are hooked-lipped browsers. The southern white rhino's square lip allows it to bite off grass close to the nutritious roots. Southern white rhinos are different in another way, as well—they prefer to live in herds, instead of a solitary existence. Understanding this behavioral trait was one of the factors in the Wild Animal Park's enormous breeding success with this species. Because of their size, most white rhinos in zoos had lived in pairs or trios, and reproduction rates were low. But when the Wild Animal Park was built, it could house a whole herd of rhinos, and before long southern white rhinos calves were arriving regularly.

Into Africa

The next encounter on your railway tour is **East Africa**, where you will catch sight of a herd of southern white rhinos, groups of agile and fleet gazelles, fierce Cape buffaloes, and towering Uganda giraffes. You'll also discover here several water-loving antelopes, the long-faced white-bearded gnu, and the striking East African crowned crane, with its stately plumage and fancy golden headdress. Eastern Africa is a highly diverse part of the world, and the Wild Animal Park's exhibit reflects that with species native to everything from savanna, to forest, to marsh habitats.

One who walks swiftly.

That's the definition of the Arabic word *"zaráfa,"* from which we derive the name giraffe. This graceful and unmistakable animal is the tallest mammal on Earth, reaching heights of up to 17 feet as adults. Even the calves are taller than many people, measuring six feet at birth. The extraordinarily long neck is the giraffes' adaptation for reaching the leaves, flowers, and shoots at the tops of trees, a food resource almost exclusively theirs. Oddly enough, they have the same number of vertebrae in their necks as humans do—seven—but each one is much larger than ours. Although the lattice pattern of their coats is variable, you can usually tell the difference between subspecies of giraffes by the size and shape of the patches. Reticulated giraffes have large reddish brown patches that are close together; Maasai giraffes have brown, irregularly shaped, "lacy" patches that continue down their legs; and the Uganda giraffe *Giraffa camelopardalis rothschildi,* seen here, has squared, reddish patches on a light background, with white on the belly.

Don't cross this fellow!

The **Cape buffalo** *Syncerus caffer caffer* has a notoriously bad temper and won't hesitate to use it. These massive and aggressive herd animals are highly defensive of their territory, mates, and young, and they have been known to attack and kill predators like lions, leopards, and hyenas, and even humans if provoked. Both sexes of the Cape buffalo carry the large, sharp horns, although they become thicker and heavier on the males.

Dance of the cranes.

The sight of several East African crowned cranes *Balearica regulorum gibbericeps* performing a courtship dance together is as graceful, elegant, and mesmerizing as any ballet. These beautifully colored birds with their decorative crowns hop, prance, and leap—sometimes as high as four feet in the air—with their wings outstretched and finish with a slow and delicate placement of their feet. They even perform a bird tap-dance while searching for food—they stamp their feet to flush locusts, grasshoppers, reptiles, and frogs out of the grass and reeds.

Anyone for a swim?

When you think of antelope, you probably think of grasslands or forests. But the East African sitatunga *Tragelaphus spekii spekii* is a semi-aquatic antelope that spends most of its time in the dense reed beds of swamps and marshes. It has widely splayed hooves for walking in mud and floating vegetation, and it is a good swimmer, crossing deep water to move from one feeding site to another in search of grasses and reeds like papyrus. To escape from predators, the sitatunga may even completely submerge and remain underwater with only its nostrils exposed to breathe.

A cool melon on a hot day.

Fringe-eared oryxes *Oryx gazella callotis* are specially adapted to survive in their African desert environment. They know to dig out shallow depressions in the ground to find a cooler place to rest, they can sense rainstorms from far away and move toward them to find new plant growth, and they have unusual circulation systems in their heads to cool their blood. They also can go without drinking water for several days, and they seek out wild melons that grow in their habitat called cucurbits, from which they obtain moisture.

A giant among herons.

At a little over five feet tall, the goliath heron *Ardea goliath* is the largest of the heron species. Its size allows it to wade into deeper waters than other birds in search of fish, so it is rarely in competition with other herons for food. Yet other heron species regularly mob together to harass the goliath—perhaps its sheer size stigmatizes it as a bully.

Of synchronicity and lunar cycles.

The Kenya impala *Aepyceros melampus rendilis* is one of the most hunted prey animals in **Africa**. Large numbers of the newborn calves are taken by predators each breeding season. So what's a mother to do to make sure the population goes on? For impalas, there truly is safety in numbers. The females have been found to synchronize conceptions, apparently based on the cycles of the moon, so that all the females in a herd give birth at about the same time. That way, there are many newborns, which can be defended more readily, and there is a strong likelihood that a good number of them will survive.

Hoofing it.

Travel is a way of life for the eastern white-bearded gnu *Connochaetes taurinus albojubatus*. Rather than establishing particular territories, the herds stay on the move as they graze. During the breeding season, a large herd is composed of smaller units containing a dominant bull and the females he defends. The rest of the year, the females move together freely without being herded by the males. The total number of gnus in an aggregate herd can reach tens and even hundreds of thousands. This is considered one of the most awe-inspiring sights in Africa: the seasonal migration of vast numbers through the Serengeti, as they travel between feeding and watering grounds.

Location is everything.

For a male Thomson's gazelle *Gazella thomsonii thomsonii*, the location of his property determines both his status and the success of his love life. As with most gazelles, Thomson's gazelle males establish and defend territories and breed with females that wander through. In order to breed with as many females as possible, and therefore carry on his genes, the male must have something to offer that will entice females. The most dominant male usually gets the territory with a pool or stream for water and good grazing for food, and the females spend a lot of time in his area. But other males may have shady trees in their territories, or a patch of particularly good grass, or a soft sandy spot to lie in, and the females will choose to join one of them for a while. And when opportunity knocks, these males are ready.

Cruise along the Nile.

They don't travel in boats, but Nile lechwes *Kobus megaceros* do spend most of their lives wandering the floodplains along the Nile River. Lechwes are the most aquatic of the grazing antelopes, feeding on river grasses and spending large amounts of time in water sometimes up to their backs. They are noted for moving in a series of leaps through water that is too shallow for swimming, and their hooves are elongated for good balance in their liquid environment.

The roar of a...deer?

Despite its delicate appearance, a male Barbary red deer *Cervus elaphus barbarus* produces a resounding roar to announce ownership rights of its rutting territory. This call also serves to announce his presence to females. Found in many parts of the world, red deer have been associated with humans for centuries. They have been depicted in prehistoric cave paintings; they've inspired many hunting rituals, legends, and lore; and at various times in history, particularly in Europe, landowners and overlords controlled rights to hunt these deer on their property, and any poachers that were caught were put to death.

Barbary red deer

Beestly looking.

The awkward appearance of the Jackson's hartebeest *Alcelaphus buselaphus jacksoni* is reflected in its common name. The word hart refers to a male deer, and the long slender face and limbs of the hartebeest do look like those of a deer. Yet its sloping body, with shoulders higher than the haunches, looks similar to the wildebeest—hence the word beest. Despite its rather clumsy physique, this rare antelope species can run at about 45 miles per hour, faster than many domestic horses.

Land of the Sahara

Soon you find yourself in the territory of **North Africa**, a 30-acre exhibit home to such diverse species as Barbary red deer, Ankole cattle, and sand gazelles. The northern part of the African continent is largely covered with desert, and the species found in this range are specially adapted to survive those harsh and challenging conditions.

Throwing extinction a curve.

The scimitar-horned oryx *Oryx dammah* is a clear example of how important captive breeding programs can be in saving endangered species. This oryx with the gracefully curved horns is critically endangered in the wild, a victim of uncontrolled hunting, agricultural encroachment, droughts, and competition for food with domestic livestock. Yet it is one of the most common antelope species in captivity, with more than 500 cared for in U.S. zoos and managed by the American Association of Zoos and Aquariums, and 700 to 1,000 in other zoos and parks in various countries. Its conservation is truly dependent on places like the Wild Animal Park, which, at this printing, has had 487 births over the years.

Hiding in plain sight.

Things are not always as they seem. The Sudan Barbary sheep *Ammotragus lervia blainei* is not actually a sheep, but it isn't a goat, either. Barbary sheep have characteristics of both, and they have been placed in their own unique genus. They live in rough, rocky, and arid country, where few plants grow that are tall enough to hide them. So they have developed an exceptional ability to hide in the open by freezing and remaining motionless whenever they sense danger. Their tawny coats blend in with the backdrop of their desert surroundings, and a predator just may pass them by.

Across shifting sands.

The nomadic sand gazelle *Gazella subgutturosa marica* has wide hooves to help it walk and run on the loose, deep sand of its habitat in the Sahara Desert. It is also the lightest in color of all the gazelles, an adaptation that reflects light so the animal doesn't overheat. The sand gazelle is also a master of taking advantage of any shade—even the thinnest shadow from a shrub is an opportunity to cool off.

Above it all.

The ostrich *Struthio camelus* has evolved with the same advantage that many hoofed stock have: long, thin legs that support its weight well above the ground and allow it to run swiftly away from danger. The African ostrich is a giant among birds, with males reaching heights of nine feet and weighing more than 300 pounds. Its large, loosely feathered wings are not used for flight—ostriches cannot fly—but they are used in a fluttering, fanning, and bowing courtship dance. The male is the home builder in this species, making a nest to entice the female to lay her eggs with him. The first female to do so becomes his "main hen," but several other subordinate females will also lay their eggs near his nest. Some of these may be incubated along with those of the first hen, but most are not. The male and the female both incubate the eggs, with the male usually taking the night shift.

Ostrich curiosity.

On Safari

A family stroll.

As you pass by the North African plains, be sure to look to your right. There you'll encounter one side of the 90-acre **South Africa** enclosure. South Africa provides views of some familiar animals—many seen in safari movies and documentaries throughout the years—such as reticulated giraffes, sable antelopes, blesboks, and waterbucks. There is a striking variety of wildlife here, including attention-getting birds like the secretary bird, wattled cranes, white-backed vultures, Dalmatian pelicans, and the South African ostrich, the world's largest living bird. You may also catch sight of the Wild Animal Park's three northern white rhinos, a highly endangered rhino subspecies that the Park hopes to breed in captivity.

Rear defense.

Hartmann's mountain zebras *Equus zebra hart-mannae* primarily live in harem groups, composed of a dominant male and several females with their young offspring. Whenever danger threatens, the male sends out a high-pitched alarm call and herds the group together, then places himself at the back. One of the females leads the others away while the male provides protection against the threat. And with a kick powerful enough to kill a lion, this zebra has earned its stripes when it comes to defense.

Snake hunter.

The secretary bird *Sagittarius serpentarius* is so unusual that it has its own family, in which it is the only species. Sometimes described as a cross between a raptor and a stork, the secretary bird is classified as a raptor—a bird of prey—because of its sharp, hooked beak and because it eats animals. It eats all kinds of things, such as grasshoppers and other insects, rodents and other small mammals, and snakes and lizards, which it captures in the African grasslands by stalking them along the ground, striding on its long legs. This bird is perhaps most famous for eating snakes, which it stamps on with its feet and sharp claws before snapping them up in its beak. This habit led to its scientific name, which means "the archer of serpents." The bird's appearance provided its common name—the long feathers on the back of its head resemble the feather writing quills that old-time secretaries used.

Clean sweep.

The South African sable antelope *Hippotragus niger niger* has some of the most magnificent horns of the African antelopes, particularly the males. The horns sweep back from the head in a pronounced curve and can be 40 inches long. It's easy to tell the males and females apart in this species, because they are very different in color: the males are a rich sable brown to black, while the females are reddish brown.

Heavy necking.

Among giraffes, like the reticulated giraffe *Giraffa camelopardalis reticulata* (below), necking means something very different than it does to humans—it's an aggressive display, instead of a display of affection. Male giraffes, particularly young bulls, swing their necks and heads at one another, often hitting rather hard, to establish dominance (bottom). Females are more cooperative with one another, however, which aids in survival. They give birth to their calves at about the same time, in traditional calving grounds that may have been used repeatedly over many years. The calves then stay together in a group known as a "creche," and the mothers take turns watching over them—the giraffe version of a day-care center.

Is time running out?

The northern white rhino *Ceratotherium simum cottoni* is one of the most endangered animals in the world. There are only about 36 of them left in the wild, 30 of which live in **Garamba National Park**. Like the southern subspecies, these rhinos are square-lipped grazers with two horns, but unlike the southern white rhino, captive breeding and reintroduction efforts have not been very successful. Because the **Wild Animal Park** has had such huge success with the southern rhinos, it was chosen as a site to receive three of the precious northern rhinos in hopes that they would breed. This has not been the case so far, which may be due in part to the lack of a large enough herd to stimulate breeding behavior. But the scientists at the **Zoological Society's Center for Reproduction of Endangered Species (CRES)** have not given up hope and are continuing to study and work with the **Wild Animal Park's** three individuals.

Head bangers: Two Uganda giraffes take a swing at one another.

He's an odd bird.

Like other cranes, the wattled crane *Bugeranus carunculatus* is a tall bird with a long neck and long legs, which it uses to wade through marshes in search of food. But unlike other cranes, it has two pendulous wattles at its throat that are thought to play a part in courtship displays. The bird's species name, *carunculatus*, means "little bits of flesh" and refers to the bumps of skin around the face. And the wattled crane has yet another odd distinction: its wattles, usually bare on most birds, are completely feathered.

The ultimate environmentalists.

African white-backed vultures *Gyps africanus* are a common sight in savanna country and open plains. They feed on carrion, and a large group of 100 can strip a 110-pound carcass in 3 minutes. Along with other vultures, they are the clean-up crew of the bird world, environmentalists that recycle the remains that no one else will touch. Vultures are often accused of killing and infecting livestock, but they don't do either: they only feed on dead animals, and they dispose of them before any bacteria can spread and do harm to other creatures, including humans. Instead of hating or fearing vultures, we should celebrate them for their vital role in the environment.

Greasy kobs.

As you might guess from its common name, the ellipsen waterbuck *Kobus ellipsiprymnus ellipsiprymnus* is never far from water. It needs to drink more than most other bovids because it eats a high-protein diet of grasses, reeds, and aquatic vegetation. This waterbuck's scientific name reveals its other characteristics, as well. *Kobus*, which comes from the native name Koba, led to the French name for these animals, *cobe onctueux*, meaning "greasy kob," because their coats are covered with an oily, musky secretion. And *ellipsiprymnus* refers to one of the best ways to identify them: they have an elliptical white circle around their rear ends.

A pod of pelicans.

Eastern white pelicans *Pelecanus onocrotalus* nest in large colonies on the ground, often with the nests only inches apart. There are frequent squabbles among neighbors, but year after year they return to the same site and do it all over again. Both the male and the female share incubation duties, wrapping the eggs in their large, webbed feet or tucking them into the breast feathers for warmth. One parent tends the nest while the other is out feeding on fish, then they exchange a brief greeting display before changing places.

Social scavengers.

In the wild, western Rueppell's vultures *Gyps rueppelli rueppelli* nest along cliff edges in colonies that can contain hundreds of these birds of prey. Because they live in large groups, they feed almost exclusively on large carrion animals, which they find by soaring aloft on warm air currents and scanning the ground below. They also watch the movements of other birds, and if they see some descending, they will head down to the site as well. They chase smaller vulture species away from the carcass, but they, in turn, can be intimidated by the larger vultures.

Rueppell's vulture

A beautiful gem.

The gemsbok *Oryx gazella gazella* is one of the oryx species, native to hot, dry country in south Africa and Namibia. It is more strikingly marked than the other species, with wide, dramatic black bands along its sides, legs, and spine. It has a long, full, and horse-like tail, undoubtedly useful for swatting flies in the heat of the day. Like the other oryxes, it travels long distances to find water and also finds moisture in acacia seed pods and wild gourds.

Family picnic.

Leadbeater's ground hornbills *Bucorvus leadbeateri* live in Africa's open grasslands, where small family groups conduct a daily patrol of their territory and spread out to methodically search the grass for food. They maintain contact with one another with frequent loud, booming calls. If a female is back at the roosting site incubating eggs or caring for chicks, the male gathers up large insects, snakes, frogs, and other tasty treats, and flies back with them to feed her and their brood. Most hornbill species seal the female into a nesting cavity in a tree to raise the chicks, but ground hornbills usually do not, choosing instead to nest among rocks or in holes they dig into earth banks.

Head in the clouds.

White-lipped deer *Cervus albirostris* are found at high elevations in Tibet and central China and have stocky, short limbs and wide, cow-like hooves to contend with a life of climbing the heights. Although their range has been fragmented because of habitat destruction, they have been found in forested and grassy areas as high as 16,000 feet. Because of their large, branching antlers, some of these deer are kept on farms in China for their antler velvet, which they shed each year as the new antlers harden. The velvet is used in traditional Chinese medicines.

Asian Hideaway

Located at the easternmost corner of the Wild Animal Park is the 35-acre **Asian Waterhole** exhibit, a boulder-strewn, grassy refuge for shy species that require a certain measure of privacy. Many of these are exotic species of deer, like Indian hog deer, Mandarin sika deer, and Père David's deer. This exhibit provides them with screened areas to get away from constant public view when they choose, as well as many hiding places to "tuck" their young. This is a common behavior among deer in which the mother chooses a safe and hidden area to leave her offspring as she ventures out to graze, then returns periodically to check on the youngster. ❧ The Asian Waterhole is also home to impressive bovid species like the Javan banteng, as well as a goat species with spectacular horns, the Turkomen markhor.

A preference for moonshine.

The Mandarin sika deer *Cervus nippon mandarinus* tends to be nocturnal in its habits, foraging for food between dusk and dawn. This may be one reason the adults keep their white spots—it helps them blend in with dappled moonlight in the forest. These shy deer do form small groups, but they are just as likely to be found living the solitary life. They are critically endangered, due to over hunting and habitat destruction, and the Wild Animal Park has been active in captive breeding efforts on their behalf. At this printing, the Park cares for a herd of 21 Mandarin sika deer and has had 8 births.

Saved by chance.

The Père David's deer *Elaphurus davidianus* of China was named after the man who described them and encouraged others to bring some to Europe, Abbe Armand David. In fact, his efforts turned out to save the species from extinction, because the majority of China's imperial herd was destroyed by a flood, then a famine, and finally hunting during the Boxer Rebellion. The last remaining Père David's deer of the imperial herd died in 1922, leaving only the individuals that had been brought to Woburn Abbey, the Duke of Bedford's estate in England. Captive-bred deer from this group were sent back to China in 1956, and there are now two reintroduced wild populations there.

The barking deer.

When it senses a predator, the North Indian muntjac *Muntiacus muntijak vaginalis* makes a deep, sharp sound like the bark of a dog, and—amazingly similar to that retriever next door—it will bark for an hour if the intruder doesn't go away. Because the muntjac is solitary, the call is also thought to announce its presence to other muntjacs nearby. If a predator insists upon pursuing the muntjac, it has yet another dog-like defense: the upper canine teeth of the male grow out into sharp, curved tusks, which the deer can use to stab its attacker.

Bellow of the bulls.

As its appearance suggests, the lowland wisent *Bison bonasus bonasus* is related to the American bison that we know so well in the United States. And just as the American bison was endangered at one time, so now is the lowland wisent, with only about 3,000 found in captivity and certain areas of the Bialowieza Forest. These huge animals, weighing between 700 and 1,500 pounds, feed on the leaves, twigs, and bark of trees and are usually found in small groups. Competition between the bulls during the rutting season can be fierce—they ram heads much like sheep and goats and emit a distinctive bellow that can be heard three miles away. And the cows have a sneaky trick to insure they get the best bull possible: even when a cow has been claimed, she may run past other bulls to stir up yet another competition.

Just resting their eyes.

Languid as they may seem, domestic cattle don't sleep much, and neither do wild cattle species like the Javan banteng *Bos javanicus javanicus*. Studies have shown that cattle only sleep from 2 to 10 minutes at a time, and they only sleep a total of about 1 hour in 24. This behavior is a response to being a large and satisfying meal for predators—bovids like the banteng are always on the alert, sensing danger first through their acute sense of smell and then assessing the threat through hearing and sight. A good thing, too, because the Javan banteng is an endangered species.

And they don't even drink wine.

The first thing you notice about male Turkomen markhors *Capra falconeri heptneri* are their amazing corkscrew-spiraled horns, which can be five feet long. The males use them for fighting during mating season, and as you might imagine, the conflicts can become quite aggressive as the males lock horns, then push and twist to try and knock one another off balance. Those horns have also been part of the decline of this endangered goat species, unfortunately, because they are prized as trophies. The goats have also been hunted for meat during military occupations, and their habitat—a limited area where Turkmenistan, Uzbekistan, Tajikistan, and Afghanistan meet—has been lost to agriculture and domestic livestock.

Here's looking at you, kid.

Siberian ibex *Capra ibex sibirica* **kids are cute, fleet-footed little critters that can already jump on the day they are born. At four weeks of age, they start goat kindergarten, spending most of their time with a group of other ibex kids from the herd and only returning to mom periodically to nurse. Although just as agile in their rocky, high-altitude world, the adults engender a bit more respect. Their heavy, thick, and ridged horns can reach lengths of four feet in the males, and during conflicts over mates, the resounding clashes of males rearing up and crashing down head-to-head are impressive.**

Getting a jump on life: a young Siberian ibex.

Climb Every Mountain

After rounding the Asian Waterhole, look up to your left to discover the **Mountain Habitat**, a rocky refuge for Siberian ibex, Himalayan tahr, and European mouflon. These agile and nimble-footed goat and sheep species are right at home on the rugged crags, which are very much like the mountainous habitats they would inhabit in the wild.

A Renaissance bovine.

With great confidence and skill, the Himalayan tahr *Hemitragus jemlahicus* bounds over the rugged hills and mountain slopes of the Himalayas where it feeds on seeds, fruits, bark, and new growth of grasses and brush. The shaggy mane on the neck and shoulders—somewhat reminiscent of the ruffled collars worn in the Renaissance—helps to keep the animal warm in frigid winter temperatures. Although it looks similar to goat species, it does not have a beard, its horns are smaller, and it has scent glands on its feet, which is probably an adaptation to announce its whereabouts to fellow tahrs in its uneven and unpredictable environment.

Clash of the Titans.

During rutting season, booming crashes echo through hills and canyons as male European mouflon sheep *Ovis orientalis musimon* butt heads in contests over females. This ritual mating behavior is the reason male sheep are called "rams." Despite the alarming sounds these clashes produce, there are rarely any serious injuries. The large, thick, curved horns of the sheep, along with a fortified skull, are designed to absorb enormous impact with little lasting effect. Even though they look nothing like the ones in Little Bo Peep's flock, mouflon sheep are considered to be the precursors of our domesticated sheep.

Making a comeback.

The Przewalski's horse *Equus przewalskii*, also called the Mongolian wild horse, was considered extinct in the wild by 1970. But this regal horse is a notable example of how a species can be saved from extinction by captive breeding in zoos and wildlife parks. Several herds of Przewalski's horses were established in captivity, one at the Wild Animal Park, and international breeding efforts gradually increased the captive population. At this printing, there are more than 1,000 Przewalski's horses maintained in 129 zoos and field stations, and reintroduced herds are holding their own in reserves in China and Mongolia.

Wild Horses

Ａs you pass by the other side of the South Africa habitat, look over to the enclosure called the **Mongolian Steppe**. Here resides the Wild Animal Park's herd of Przewalski's horses, the last species of wild horse left in the world. They are descendants of the horses depicted in the ancient cave paintings at Lascaux, France, and they are an endangered species that has been the subject of international conservation efforts since the 1950s. 🐾 Information exchange and breeding loans between Russia, China, the United States, and Europe have brought this magnificent species back from the brink of extinction, and today, efforts are underway to reintroduce these horses to their traditional Asian homeland.

Horsing around.

The playful antics of Przewalski's horse foals is always an enjoyable sight, as they gallop, kick, and sidle up to one another. Every birth of this endangered species is cause for celebration, and the Zoological Society has celebrated 116 times.

Social gathering.

A typical herd of Przewalski's horses contains a dominant stallion, several mares and their young offspring, and perhaps one or two young, subordinate males tolerated by the stallion. These wild horses are very social, seeking out one another's company, exchanging whinnies, and grooming one another by nibbling with their teeth.

Making love, not war.

The bonobo *Pan paniscus* has also been called the pygmy chimpanzee, but this is a misnomer—bonobos are a different species and have many unique characteristics, they are not just smaller versions of common chimpanzees. One of their most famous differences is that they prefer to solve conflicts with food sharing and sexual contact, instead of physical fights. They also tend not to form raiding parties and attack neighboring chimpanzee groups, as common chimps are known to do.

Primate Paradise

As you pass by the far end of East Africa, look to your left for a grassy knoll called **Bonobo Hill**. Here resides the Wild Animal Park's troop of bonobos, also known as pygmy chimpanzees. Visitors may or may not see these energetic primates—the bonobos are fickle that way. Their two-acre enclosure is designed with two parts, one in front of the hill where they can sit and peruse the railway as it goes by (one wonders, who is watching whom?), and the other behind the hill, where the troop can enjoy a leisurely afternoon in privacy. Of course, you might spy some of the youngsters up in a palm tree, as well, trying out their agility and acrobatic skills.
🐾 This is almost the conclusion of your Wgasa Bush Line Railway tour, as the train winds its way back to Nairobi Village, passing by Heart of Africa and affording some spectacular views.

Great apes.

Bonobos share between 98.5 and 98.9 percent of their DNA with humans, and they share many of our behaviors as well. They are caring and attentive parents that teach their offspring both survival and societal skills, they use tools to obtain food and modify their environment, and they act cooperatively for the good of the entire troop. Of course they have their bad days, too, and will scream, bite, and hit to make a point. You may have experienced a staff meeting or family gathering like that at one time or another....

Playtime.

Infant bonobos are born relatively helpless and must be carried everywhere. The young stay close to their mothers for several years while they grow and learn the ropes, although they form bonds with other members of the troop as well. Playing is an important part of growing up, as the young bonobos gain independence and test their skills against one another. The Wild Animal Park has had eight bonobo births since 1989, and because this species—like all the great apes—is endangered, each birth is a happy event.

A good thrashing.

The eastern giant eland *Taurotragus der-*
bianus gigas **lives in open woodlands in**
Africa and feeds on leaves and fruits,
which it obtains by thrashing the trees.
It uses its long, spiraled horns to pull
down branches of the munondo tree
Isoberlinia globiflora, **and twists its head**
vigorously to shake out any fruit.
Despite its large size—about 5 feet at
the shoulder, 11 feet long, and weighing
about 1,000 pounds—the giant eland is
quite agile and can leap over a 5-foot
barrier with ease.

And There's More!

If you think you've seen it all upon disembarking from the railway tour, you're pleasantly mistaken. The Wild Animal Park has much more to offer, with short jaunts or longer treks into some truly unique exhibit areas. Intrepid adventurer that you are, it's time to stretch those legs and take a walk on the wild side. Of course, you could also begin your Wild Animal Park adventure with these exhibits, and finish up with the railway tour. Just as for the animals, your choices and opportunities abound!

Hidden in the shadows.

The shy and secretive okapi *Okapia johnstoni* **was unknown to western scientists until 1901, when an explorer by the name of Sir Harry Johnston discovered the animals in their dense rain forest home in Africa. Although their beautiful coats are boldly patterned and look conspicuous to us, they are perfect camouflage in the shadows and streaks of light in the okapis' native environment. Because of the black-and-white stripes on the hindquarters, many people think that okapis are related to zebras, but they are actually related to giraffes. If you look closely, you can see the resemblance in the shape of the head and the knobby horns.**

A Walking Safari

The heart and soul of Africa is its amazing diversity of species, which includes some of the most widely recognized and admired animals in the world. The Wild Animal Park has captured the enduring spirit of Africa's wild places in its **Heart of Africa** exhibit, which first opened in May 1997. Heart of Africa is a walking safari that will bring you close to such majestic animals as okapis, bonteboks, giraffes, and cheetahs. ❧ The three-quarter-mile walking trail that begins at the southern end of Nairobi Village takes you from the forest to the savanna to a serene lake by means of rustic paths, wooden-planked walkways, and even a floating bridge. The winding trails and gentle terrain offer many places to sit beneath the trees or near the streams, and side trips abound, as if you had ventured off the beaten path in the African plains. You'll even encounter an island research station, to get a glimpse of the field researcher's lifestyle. ❧ This is a magical journey that will transport you to the Heart of Africa, a safari—which means "travel" in Swahili—that is as much spiritual as it is physical.

Forward leap.

With a purplish, glossy sheen to their coats and contrasting white markings, bonteboks *Damaliscus pygargus pygargus* make a bold statement on the southern African savanna. Although they may look a bit ungainly as they run, they are swift animals that can reach speeds of up to 40 miles per hour. They jump well, too, and can be seen leaping over each other's backs if suddenly alarmed. These antelope were almost hunted to extinction by 1830, but protected herds were maintained in private and government parks, and the wild population is now about 2,000 animals.

The hunted becomes the hunter.

Forest-dwelling duikers are prey for leopards, eagles, and humans. But they are unique in the antelope world, because they not only eat plants, they also eat other animals—and they even actively hunt them. A large part of their diet includes fruits, leaves, and bark, but they also eat insects, frogs, and reptiles, and they have been observed hunting for small mammals and birds. They kill their prey by biting it or stamping on it. The yellow-backed duikers *Cephalophus sylvicultor sylvicultor* found in the Park's Heart of Africa are the largest of the duiker species, and are easily identified by the yellow hair on the rump and along the spine that stands up straight when the duiker is startled.

Yellow-backed duiker

Taking their time.

East African kori bustards *Ardeotis kori struthiunculus* are large, ground-dwelling birds that live on Africa's open grasslands. They feed on insects and small reptiles, finding their food by taking a leisurely, meandering walk through the grass to stir up dinner. The common name bustard is a combination of two French words, *outarde* and *bistarde*, and can be translated to mean "a slow walking bird." Male bustards are well known for their courtship displays, and the Kori bustard's version is to puff out its throat and feathers to form a large, ruffled sac, while it spreads out and droops its wings, forming a fan.

The better to hear you with.

The first thing you think about the South African bat-eared fox *Otocyon megalotis megalotis* is that it must have extraordinary hearing —and it does. Those enormous ears, up to 5 inches long on a fox that stands 15 inches high, are extremely sensitive and are used primarily to find food. That's even more remarkable when you know what bat-eared foxes eat: termites! The foxes can actually hear harvester termites moving underground, and catch them by digging up their nest. Bat-eared foxes look comical as they meander through the grass, stopping often to tilt their ears toward the ground, but their talent for finding such small prey is something few animals can match.

Fine swine.

Some people say it has a face only a mother could love. Others say it's so ugly it's cute. But pig-lovers say that the African warthog *Phacochoerus africanus* is a swine of nobility and distinction. So why the warts? Males have two prominent sets of these fleshy protuberances, females have only one less-conspicuous set, and they serve as padding during fights. This is the most-watched pig in Africa, and safari travelers are familiar with the lines of sows and piglets trotting along with their tasseled tails in the air. Warthogs take refuge in burrows, which they back into in order to greet an assailant with their sharp tusks at the ready.

"When I'm calling you..."

One of several noticeable characteristics of Kikuyu colobus monkeys *Colobus guereza kikuyuensis* is their habit of calling loudly together, a roaring chorus from each troop that occurs at dawn and again at night, and sometimes in between when the troop plans to move. These calls keep the troop together and also announce its presence to other colobus nearby. If two troops meet, there is hostility and fighting, so they are more comfortable knowing each other's locations to avoid run-ins. Kikuyu colobus are a distinctive sight in the forest, because of their black-and-white coloring, their sweeping mantles of long white hair, and their long, white-tufted tails. Forest travelers are most likely to see the tails first, hanging down through the branches.

Built for speed.

South African cheetahs *Acinonyx jubatus jubatus* are famous for sprinting up to 70 miles per hour to catch their prey and are considered the fastest animals on land. They are uniquely built for these bursts of speed, with large nostrils and lungs to take in more oxygen, and long legs and a flexible spine for a huge stride. They also have narrow, dog-like paws with hard, thick pads that absorb shock and provide great traction. And unlike all other cats, their claws are only semi-retractable and are thick and blunt to grab the ground as they run. Cheetahs are an endangered species, and the Zoological Society has been involved in conservation efforts for them since 1972. The CRES Cheetah Breeding Facility at the Wild Animal Park is part of a cooperative program among zoos for captive breeding, and at this printing 116 cheetahs have been born at the Park.

Pretty in pink.

The lesser flamingo *Phoeniconaias minor* is not the deep salmon color of the Carribean flamingo but rather a soft pink with a streak of darker pink feathers in the wings. Why are flamingos that color? It's the carotene pigment in the food they eat, particularly in algae. In captivity, foods such as carrots, peppers, and shrimp have been added to the birds' diet to maintain their rosy color, which is important in choosing mates. The pink can fade in sunlight, however, and adult flamingos can also look white when they are feeding chicks, because the adults are eating less. While lesser flamingos usually don't breed well in captivity, the Park's flock is a happy exception to the rule.

A greater flamingo *Phoenicopterus ruber roseus* sifts for supper.

Revered bird.

In ancient Egypt, the African sacred ibis *Threskiornis aethiopicus aethiopicus* was indeed sacred, because it was the symbol of Thoth, the god of writing and wisdom. This bird was worshiped and kept in temples, and it was so highly revered that even wild ibises were mummified upon their deaths and buried in special animal necropolises. However, the sacred ibis has not been seen in Egypt since the mid-19th century, killed in more recent times for its feathers and displaced by the destruction of its marsh and swamp habitats. Today the sacred ibis is only found south of the Sahara in Africa.

The thunderbird rises again.

The California condor *Gymnogyps californianus* once ranged over much of the western and southern United States, and it was known as the powerful thunderbird to some Native American tribes. But by 1987, the entire world population of California condors numbered only 27 birds, and the last remaining wild condor was brought into captivity to try and save the species from extinction. Things looked bleak for these magnificent vultures, but with specialized breeding and hand-raising techniques, chicks began to hatch in captivity. The first captive-bred chick, Molloko, hatched at the Wild Animal Park on April 29, 1988 to much celebration. Since then, more than 80 California condors have hatched at the Wild Animal Park, and at this printing, the world population is more than 170 birds. The success of the California Condor Recovery Program has been so great that more than 80 birds have been reintroduced into remote parts of California and Arizona.

Land of the Thunderbirds

Imagine witnessing a California condor with its impressive, nine-foot wingspan as it glides on thermal air currents from a canyon below. It's a breathtaking sight, and one that you may see for yourself at the Wild Animal Park's **Condor Ridge**. This habitat tells the stories of native North American species that have experienced both decline and recovery, compelling tales of survival that have much to teach us about caring for our native wildlife heritage. ✳ Your journey of discovery begins in the Conifer Arboretum, taking you past beautiful thick-billed parrots and northern aplomado falcons, as well as the burrows of black-tailed prairie dogs, black-footed ferrets, and western burrowing owls. You'll then come upon a viewing deck with spectacular sights of bighorn sheep and, of course, the legendary thunderbirds themselves, the California condors. Telescopic viewing, interpretive video, and an interactive electronic map will add to your understanding of the amazing wildlife we have in our own backyard.

Snow birds.

It's odd to see tropical-looking thick-billed parrots *Rhynchopsitta pachyrhyncha* foraging in a layer of snow, but in the wild these cold-weather parrots live in high-altitude conifer forests and feed on the seeds of pine cones. At one time their range included Arizona and New Mexico, but due to hunting, trapping, and habitat destruction, thick-billed parrots were no longer seen in the U.S. by the 1930s. Today they are only found in the mountain ranges of northwest and central Mexico. But conservation efforts are underway, and the Wild Animal Park is participating in the captive-breeding effort with its lively and noisy parrots at Condor Ridge.

What a pair.

The northern aplomado falcon *Falco femoralis septentrionalis* uses the buddy system when hunting its prey of doves and cuckoos—a mated pair hunts cooperatively, with the male falcon attacking and chasing the bird into a tree and the female falcon swooping in to flush it out. These falcons also eat insects that they snap up in mid-air. Both parents take part in raising the chicks, although the female does all the incubating while the male defends the nest site and brings her food. Aplomado falcons are found in parts of Mexico, Central America, and South America, although their range used to extend into Arizona, New Mexico, and Texas. In the 1980s and 1990s, efforts were made to reintroduce this beautiful bird of prey to the U.S., and further releases are planned for the future.

Our town.

Black-tailed prairie dogs *Cynomys ludovi-cianus* **are a social bunch and live in extensive systems of underground bur-rows called towns. A town can cover 140 square miles and contain more than one million prairie dogs. But these towns are not freely connected by tunnels—they are divided first into "wards," sort of like our neighborhoods, and then again into "coteries," which are akin to our houses or apartment buildings. The prairie dogs in a coterie all know one another well and reinforce their bonds by kissing, nuz-zling, grooming one another, and playing together. They also defend and clean up their burrows, and they pay particular attention to those mounds of dirt at the tunnel entrances, which keep water from flooding the burrows and provide ventila-tion. But if the prairie dogs of one coterie meet up with those of another, even though they're in the same town, there's likely to be a fight. Just goes to show, you can't always trust your neighbors—not even in the rodent world.**

Beep, beep!

Western greater roadrunners *Geococcyx californianus californianus* get their name from their habit of speeding along the ground, at up to 15 miles per hour, to catch food and escape danger. They can fly, but they prefer to run. This is probably because their food is close to the ground—roadrunners are aggressive predators, not vegetarians, and they eat insects, lizards, mice, scorpions, and even small rattlesnakes that they snatch up in their dry, brush-covered terrain. The desert-dwelling birds have a fascinating technique to cool off on extremely hot days: they vibrate their throats to move air rapidly past the moist tissues of their respiratory system, like their own internal fan.

Linked destinies.

Black-footed ferrets *Mustela nigripes* live on the same North American grasslands as prairie dogs. The ferrets depend upon these rodents as a food source and as the architects that build their homes—they use the same underground burrows and tunnels. Widespread eradication of prairie dogs has severely hurt the black-footed ferret population, and in the late 1980s the ferrets became extinct in the wild. Captive breeding of these small carnivores brought their numbers up to 400 by 1996, and several groups have since been reintroduced in Wyoming, Montana, South Dakota, and Arizona.

Slow and steady wins the race.

The desert tortoise *Gopherus agassizi* may amble slowly through life, but that life is long. Like all tortoises, desert tortoises can live as long as 150 years. Native to the hot, dry deserts of the southwestern United States and northeastern Mexico, these reptiles cope with the heat by digging deep underground burrows to rest in, a habit that gives them the genus name *Gopherus* and the nickname gopher tortoises. Other animals use their burrows as well, like gopher snakes and burrowing owls.

Gone underground.

Not all owls spend their time aloft, flying the night skies and roosting in trees. The western burrowing owl *Athene cunicularia hypugaea* lives in underground burrows. It can dig its own, but it usually takes over the burrows of prairie dogs or desert tortoises. It also tends to hunt for food in the daylight, hopping along the ground on its long legs to snap up insects. Some of these insects end up stored in the burrow, a stockpile for leaner days. During cold winters, burrowing owls slow down their metabolism, breathing, and heart rate to conserve energy. Because they live on the ground, burrowing owls are vulnerable to a variety of predators, but they have developed a rather amazing way to deal with a threat: they can produce a call that sounds like a rattlesnake.

Strength in numbers.

Most birds of prey prefer a solitary life or a single partner, but western Harris' hawks *Parabuteo unicinctus superior* like to be social. They live in groups of four to seven hawks, usually close relatives of varying ages, and they hunt cooperatively for their prey of rabbits, squirrels, and small birds. They've even been observed using relay hunting, in which one bird picks up where another leaves off in chasing the prey. This strategy allows each bird to expend less energy and makes it possible for the group to feed on larger animals than one hawk could catch alone. The family unit is an advantage in raising chicks, as well—the breeding pair mate and lay the eggs, their subordinate "helpers" hunt and bring back food, and they all defend the nest.

My, what big horns you have!

In desert bighorn sheep *Ovis canadensis cremnobates* society, horn size equals status. The bigger a male's horns are, the more dominant he is, and the more territory and females he controls. The massive, spiral horns have an average length of 3½ feet and readily subdue a subordinate male's enthusiasm during a fight. Desert bighorn sheep have remarkable eyesight and are excellent climbers and jumpers, a skill they make daily use of in their rocky mountainside habitat. Yet because of fragmentation of that habitat and hunting by humans, they are endangered. Because bighorn sheep form home ranges based on guidance from the herd they were born into, they are not likely to wander far in search of new habitat. This makes them vulnerable to disturbance, and the smaller the area of habitat, the less reproduction that occurs in the herd—a vicious circle that threatens the existence of the species. The Zoological Society of San Diego has been working in conjunction with several organizations to study the desert bighorn sheep and learn more about its social structure and habitat use, so that the Species Survival Plan for this animal can take steps to protect it and increase its population.

Epiphyllum "Euphorsene"

Botanical Beauties

Epiphyllum "Tropical Cactus"

Up the way from Condor Ridge is a path that will take you to some of the most spectacular sights in San Diego, at the **Kupanda Falls Botanical Center**. Here you will find shady refuges like the Epiphyllum House, the Fuchsia House, and the Bonsai Pavilion, as well as various specialized gardens of rare, unusual, and little-known botanical wonders. Look here for the Old World Succulent Garden, the Baja Garden, and the California Nativescapes Garden. ❧ In addition, there are gardens in other parts of the Park, including the fragrant Herb Garden on the walking trail near Kilima Point, the colorful and oddly shaped blooms of the Protea Garden on the trail near the lions, the large Conifer Arboretum near Condor Ridge, and the lush greenery of the Australian Rain Forest near Heart of Africa. And these are just the formalized botanical spots. ❧ As you wander through all the many and varied delights of the Wild Animal Park, stop to notice the extraordinary representatives of the Plant Kingdom around you. Look for winter-blooming coral trees, flowering vines like wisteria and honeysuckle, thorny acacia trees, and hardy ficus trees, among many others.

Epiphyllum "Flamingo Orange"

The orchid cactus.

During the spring, especially in April and May, the Wild Animal Park's Epiphyllum House in full bloom is an unforgettable experience. Surrounded by these jewels of the tropics, you'll feel as if you wandered into a flower wonderland. These epiphyllums are hybrids of epiphytic cacti species that are native to the tropical jungles of Central and South America. These cacti grow in the forks of trees or in rock crevices and get their nourishment from decaying leaf and animal matter, and their moisture from rain and humidity in the air. The Greek word *epiphyllum* means "upon the leaf," because the flowers seem to bloom right on the leaves. But, as in other cacti, these aren't really leaves—they are flattened stems, and the flowers bud and then bloom out of them. The blossoms can range from 1 inch to 12 inches or more in diameter, and they come in a dazzling array of colors, from white, cream, pink, and rose, to orange, shades of red and deep purple, and violet, as well as the more uncommon yellow and gold. Maintained and cared for by volunteers of the San Diego Epiphyllum Society, the Park's Epiphyllum House is filled with brilliant botanical wonders.

A cactus of many colors.

Lady's eardrops.

Fuchsias are one of the world's most popular garden plants. With names like Devonshire Dumpling, Happy Wedding, Dark Eyes, and Party Frock, how could they not be? Fuchsia blossoms come in many sizes, from tiny ones the size of a peanut to giants the size of a child's fist. Their pendulous position on the stem has earned them the nickname of "lady's eardrops," and they come in a sleek single form or as a flounced and frilled double. Fuchsias were first described in the late 17th century by Father Charles Plumier, who named the plant after German botanist Leonard Fuchs. The wild species are native to Central and South America and New Zealand, and these have been extensively hybridized to produce the cultivated varieties we see today. Fuchsia popularity reached a high point during the Victorian and Edwardian eras, but fell off during the war years when greenhouses were needed to grow food. Today, fuchsias are experiencing a triumphant comeback, and you can see why during a visit to the Wild Animal Park's colorful Fuchsia House, which is cared for by an enthusiastic group of volunteers.

Bonsai Pavilion

Tiny forest.

An extraordinary blend of art and nature, bonsai growing is a tradition that began many centuries ago. First called *p'en tsi*, these diminutive and delicate trees were a favorite of the Chinese aristocracy. By the 14th century, the creation of these living sculptures had been introduced into Japan, where the growing techniques were refined into an art form. The name bonsai is made up of two Japanese words: *bon* means "tray or shallow dish," and *sai* means "plant or tree." Thus we have a tree planted in a tray. But not just any tree, and not just any tray. The proper growing of bonsai must follow strict rules. A particular style is chosen and a tree to go with it, and the choice of a pot depends on the outline of the tree and the size and appearance of its trunk. The placement of the tree in the pot is also important: a *chokkan* (formal upright tree), for example, should be planted off center. At the Wild Animal Park's Bonsai Pavilion, you can discover the amazing artistry of this part of Japanese culture, which has become a popular hobby with gardeners all over the world. An exhibit of 30 to 40 trees in a tranquil setting awaits you, cared for by members of the San Diego Bonsai Club. Some have been designed by club members, and some have been donated to the collection. In the true spirit of bonsai, they all show an appreciation of the wonders of nature.

Old World oddities.

The Wild Animal Park's Old World Succulent Garden demonstrates a fact that may surprise some gardeners: All cacti are succulents, but not all succulents are cacti. A succulent is defined as a plant that stores water in its tissues and structures. Usually the leaves or stems are modified for this storage, but sometimes it is the root or stem that is enlarged. When most people think of succulents, they think of cacti, but there are many plant species that have developed a succulent form to cope with an arid environment. These include members of the lily family, like *Aloe sessiliflora* and *Aloe striata*, some African cycads *Encephalartos* sp., and members of the euphorbia family, such as *Euphorbia ingens* and a succulent grape, *Cyphostemma juttae*. Succulent plants come in an amazing array of shapes and sizes, from 30-foot trees to tiny rosettes only 1 inch across. The Park's Old World Succulent Garden, cared for by volunteers of the San Diego Cactus and Succulent Society, is the perfect place to show off their diversity.

Aloe pluridens

Aloe thraskii

Barrel cactus *Ferocactus viridescens*

Cycad *Encephalartos ferox*

Cycad *Encephalartos umbellunziensis*

South of the border.

Baja California is a nearly 800-mile-long peninsula separated from mainland Mexico by the Sea of Cortez. It is a unique desert environment where a large variety of fascinating plant species can be found, including some that only grow on this peninsula. The Wild Animal Park's Baja Garden, cared for by volunteers of the San Diego Cactus and Succulent Society, is dedicated to displaying the wonders of Baja—the tall and short, the leafy and spiny. Among the cacti you'll find here are the old man cactus *Lophocereus schottii*, with its long stems and shaggy thatch of long, gray spines at the top; the organ pipe cactus *Myrtillocactus cochal*; and the cordon cactus *Pachycereus pringlei*, with its branching arms, which is often mistaken for the saguaro cactus of Arizona. Trees include the blue fan palm *Brahea armata*, with its arching flower spikes, and the bizarre-looking boojum *Idria columnaris*, with its curled and arched extensions. There are more than 200 boojums gracing the slopes, making the Baja Garden one of the largest collections of these rare trees outside their native habitat. Look, too, for mesquite trees *Prosopis glandulosa* and Coulter pines *Pinus coulteri*, and the pink flowers of *Euphorbia xantii*, which is, surprisingly, a relative of the Christmas poinsettia.

Cordon cactus *Pachycereus pringlei*

Boojum tree *Idria columnaris*

Douglas iris *Iris douglasiana*

In your own backyard.

Sometimes we miss extraordinary things that are right under our noses. The Wild Animal Park's California Nativescapes Botanical Garden seeks to remedy that, by showing off the beautiful plant species native to our own California habitats. Designed and cared for by volunteers of the Lake Hodges Native Plant Club, the garden is arranged to represent distinct plant communities, created in the wild by differences in elevation, rainfall, and temperature. A riparian or streamside community blooms with springtime flowers, including California fuchsias, lavender Douglas irises, pink wild roses, rose-colored hummingbird sage, and bright yellow monkey flowers. The coastal sage scrub area touts fragrant white sage, black sage, purple sage, and California sagebrush, which isn't really a sage at all but a member of the aster family. In the low desert community, look for saguaro cactus, brittlebrush, blue-flowered smoke trees, desert willows, and globemallow flowers. The high desert section shows off endangered Joshua trees, while the arger pines, manzanitas, incense cedar, and quaking aspen of the mountain community sway with the wind. Since this is a slice of California, look for native plants that decided to grow here on their own, like beardstongue, California peony, ground pinks, jimson weed, suncups, and California poppies.

Purple sage *Salvia leucophylla*

Datilillo *Yucca valida*

Beardstongue *Penstemon spectabilis*

California poppy *Eschscholtzia californica*

A taste for herbs.

Herbs have a long and rich history in culinary and medicinal use, legend, and lore. The Wild Animal Park's Herb Garden, cared for by local volunteers, provides visitors with a feast for the senses, with lovely colors, intriguing textures, and tempting fragrances. Some of the herb plants are familiar, like chili peppers, rosemary, lavender, and fennel. Some are unusual types of familiar plants, such as pine–apple or apple mint and scented geraniums like cedar geranium, apricot geranium, nutmeg geranium, or peppermint geranium. Others are less known, like borage *Borago officinalis*, called the herb of courage, which has blue, star-shaped blossoms that are edible and taste like cucumber; and love-lies-bleeding *Amaranthus caudatus*, which produces protein-rich seeds that are used as a grain. There are also roses here, since roses are considered an herb and are used in making rose water, rose syrup, rose vinegar, rose honey, rose jam, rose ice cream, crystallized rose petals, and potpourri. Even when the petals are gone, the rose hips add vitamin C to tea blends. So if you are led by the nose—or a love of history, medicine, or cooking—you'll be glad you strolled through the sensational Herb Garden.

San Pasqual rosemary *Rosmarinus officinalis*

Chocolate mint geranium *Pelargonium tomentosum*

Borage *Borago officinalis*

King protea *Protea cyanoides*

A flower of many faces.

Proteas are ornamental shrubs and trees native to Africa and Australia that have unusual flowers of many sizes, shapes, and colors. The plants are named after the Greek god Proteus, who could assume many different forms. Considered to be among the oldest flowering plants on Earth, proteas are a part of culture and folklore. The king protea *Protea cynaroides* is the national flower of South Africa, and images of protea flowers are found on coins and stamps. The Wild Animal Park's Protea Garden provides a beautiful setting to discover these many-faceted flowers, with pathways winding through buffalo grass and recessed and shaded benches where you can stop and admire the view. Along the way you'll see proteas like the sugarbush *Protea repens*, which has a sweet nectar used by early settlers to sweeten beverages and desserts, and the king protea, with its huge pink flowers 6 to 10 inches in diameter. Look for the silver tree *Leucodendron argenteum*, which can grow to 20 feet and has leaves that sparkle in the sun. There are also a variety of pincushion plants, named for the shape of their flowers. The nodding pincushion *Leucospermum cordifolium* produces masses of bright red flowers, and Catherine's pincushion *Leucospermum catherinae* has yellow flowers that resemble a pinwheel. Located south of the Kupanda Falls Botanical Center, between the Conifer Arboretum and Tiger Overlook, the Protea Garden is a rare treat.

Protea *Leucadendron discolor*

Pincushion protea *Leucospermum nutans*

What a cool place: the misty paths of the Australian Rain Forest.

A misty walk Down Under.

With dry grassland areas like the African savanna and the Asian plains represented in the Wild Animal Park's field exhibits, it is quite a surprise to come upon the Park's Australian Rain Forest, located near Heart of Africa on the Kilimanjaro Safari Walk. This garden of botanical treasures from Down Under shades a sun-dappled path as misters wet the air from the tops of the trees. Plants like the Tasmanian tree fern *Dicksonia antarctica*, the firewheel tree *Stenocarpus sinnatus*, the Queensland umbrella tree *Schefflera actinophylla*, and the white bollywood tree *Neolitsea dealbata* leave no doubt that you are in Aussie territory. But there is another surprise: You won't find many eucalyptus trees here, and eventually there will be none. Even though the gum trees are as Australian to the world as koalas, they in fact don't belong here, because most grow in temperate forests. Instead, the Park's horticulture department plans to add more plants that will accurately depict a true Australian rain forest environment, like the Moreton Bay chestnut *Castanospermum australe* and the Australian flame tree *Brachychiton sterculia*.

Tree fern *Dicksonia antarctica*

Illawarra flame tree *Brachychiton acerifolius*

Australian umbrella tree *Brassaia actinophylla*

Fall color surrounding Savannah Picnic Grove will brighten your feast.

Back Door to Discovery

There are many ways to enjoy the Wild Animal Park, and one of them gives you a truly unique perspective: a jaunt along the **Kilimanjaro Safari Walk**. This 1¾-mile, back-country path leads you to unforgettable sights and vistas. Bring your camera, wear comfortable walking shoes, and take along a picnic or snack and some water, and you're set for adventure. 🐾 There are a variety of possible routes, so take a look at your Park map and decide where you'd like to go. Spend the day exploring all the trails, or focus on one section.

If you start out on the road under the railway bridge, next to the Petting Kraal, then head to your left, you'll come upon the **Elephant Overlook**, a shady vantage point to watch the elephants for as long as you'd like, and possibly see them splashing in their pool. If you're there at the right time (check when you first enter the Park), an Elephant Encounter nearby demonstrates the elephants' husbandry behaviors and interactions with their keepers. Continue left past the elephants, and a path leads you to **Condor Ridge**, to see the California condors in their aviary exhibit, along with other threatened and endangered North American species. Then it's on up to the **Kupanda Falls Botanical Center** to see the specialty gardens. The trail winds through this colorful area and comes out near the **Conifer Arboretum** and the **Protea Garden**. Continue down the stairs to the **Tiger Overlook**, and rest on the shaded benches to read about one of the world's most endangered species. Look closely for the tigers, especially as they blend into the shade. Past the tigers, a path leads to the spectacular view at **Kilima Point**. This shaded resting spot overlooks the beautiful expanse of the East Africa field exhibit, along with the magnificent hills of the San Pasqual Valley in the background. From here, you'll head back toward Nairobi Village via the **Heart of Africa** complex and the misty wonders of the **Australian Rain Forest**, with emus, cassowaries, and rhinoceros hornbills nearby. Whether you spend an hour in one area or an entire day creating your own safari, it's a whole new view.

Look over the elephants at the Elephant Overlook.

Wear comfortable shoes and bring your camera!

Stream side: **A stroll through the Conifer Arboretum.**

The Kilimanjaro Safari Walk offers views you won't find elsewhere.

G'day mate! The path through the Australian Rain Forest.

Other Wild Adventures

With a bit of advance planning, the Wild Animal Park can also offer some exciting opportunities that are unique in Southern California. Have you ever bounced along in an open-sided truck to feed eager giraffes in Africa and sunning rhinos in Asia? Have you ever been stopped in the road by a herd of fiery-eyed Cape buffalo? How about taking your own photos of dancing crowned cranes? If not, it's time you found out what you've been missing! A **Photo Caravan** at the Wild Animal Park will give you opportunities for all this and much more. ❧ Make reservations in advance—these caravans sell out quickly—and bring your camera for a guided journey directly into the Park's field exhibits. You can't get any closer to roaming wildlife than this!

You love camping and sitting by a campfire under the stars. But have you experienced this with the roar of a lion, the trumpets of elephants, or the galloping of wildebeest to lull you to sleep? You can, at a Wild Animal Park **Roar & Snore** overnight camp. ❧ Make reservations, then bring your sleeping bag and some friends and head out to the Park's special campground overlooking the East Africa exhibit. Provided two-person tents, delicious meals around the campfire, family-oriented activities, and special animal guests all make for a memorable experience.

It's your 10th wedding anniversary—or your daughter's 12th birthday, your son's graduation, the company picnic, or a family reunion—and you want to plan a party that everyone will be talking about for weeks. Why not have it at the Wild Animal Park? The **Sales** department can help you decide on a location and all the details for an unforgettable gathering, from colorful casual buffets to black-tie, sit-down dinners by candlelight. ❧ No matter what you're celebrating, the Wild Animal Park provides a spectacular setting to make your party one of a kind.

Give me biscuits! You'll come face-to-face with animals like giraffes and Indian rhinos on a Photo Caravan.

On a **Roar & Snore Campover,** sleeping under the stars takes on a new meaning with southern white rhinos and giraffes wandering nearby.

Jambo!

We hope you have enjoyed your visit to our wildlife refuge nestled in the hills of San Pasqual Valley. The Wild Animal Park is an ever-moving, ever-changing kaleidoscope of exotic sights and sounds, with new discoveries and adventures awaiting you at each return. In the spirit and language of Africa, we say Jambo!—a Swahili word that means both goodbye and hello, because we hope to see you again soon.

Come see Hua Mei, the world-famous giant panda cub, at the Zoo's Giant Panda Research Station.

Female giant panda Bai Yun

The World-Famous San Diego Zoo

Male giant panda Shi Shi

There are sweeping savannas and hidden jungles at the Wild Animal Park, but that's not all that's wild in San Diego! ❧ In the heart of Balboa Park downtown, the San Diego Zoo is waiting to greet you with even more wonders of the natural world. Journey through more than one tropical paradise at the San Diego Zoo in Gorilla Tropics, Tiger River, the Owens Rain Forest Aviary, Sun Bear Forest, and Ituri Forest. Chill out in Polar Bear Plunge, then explore the sun-drenched rocks of the African Kopje. Children will delight in their own Children's Zoo as they discover otters, wombats, and naked mole-rats, pet a bunny or a sheep, play some games, and see shows designed just for them. The Reptile House and Reptile Mesa are a must for colorful chameleons, spiny-tailed lizards, impressive Komodo dragons, rare and endangered snakes, and those giants of the reptile world, the Galápagos tortoises. See some of the other big guys on Elephant Mesa, and be sure to look up on Horn and Hoof Mesa for the towering giraffes. The Koala Barn houses our singular collection of Queensland koalas, and discover more of Australia down the way with tree kangaroos, quolls, and Tasmanian devils. ❧ There are more than 860 animal species and more than 4,500 individual animals cared for at the San Diego Zoo, not to mention its world-class botanical collection, making it one of the best zoos in the world and a wildlife lover's dream. And when you've traveled to our representative four corners of the world, you can even enjoy sit-down, full-service gourmet dining at our lovely indoor restaurant, Alberts!

The San Diego Zoo houses the largest collection of Queensland koalas outside Australia.

Caribbean flamingos greet you on the Zoo's front plaza.

Here there be dragons: the Zoo's male Komodo dragon.

Helping a California condor hatch.

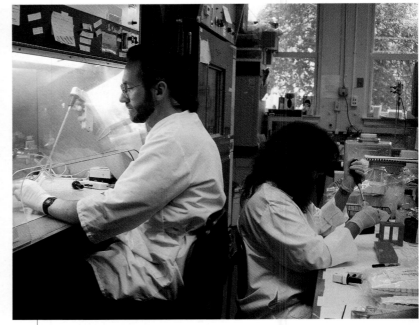

At work in the laboratory.

The Key Is Conservation

For decades, since it became clear that the world was losing its wildlife and wild places, the Zoological Society of San Diego has worked to protect threatened and endangered species. The Wild Animal Park and the San Diego Zoo have been and continue to be a vital part of that effort, contributing significantly to field research, Species Survival Plans (SSPs), and captive breeding. These contributions have not come easily, however—they are the result of years of concentrated research and the dedication of staff scientists, curators, keepers, and veterinarians. A large part of this work has been conducted at the Zoological Society's Center for Reproduction of Endangered Species (CRES), established in 1975 by Dr. Kurt Benirschke. CRES is composed of seven main divisions: Reproductive Physiology, Endocrinology, Behavior, Cytogenetics, Molecular Genetics, Ecology, and Virology. This branch of the Zoological Society employs more than 50 full-time employees and more than a dozen senior scientists, as well as lab technicians and research fellows. Their research efforts, along with those of the animal management and veterinary areas, add up to more than 80 conservation projects that the Zoological Society conducts in countries all over the world. Take a look at the map on the next two pages to locate these varied projects and see the scope of the Society's work around the globe—work that your support makes possible.

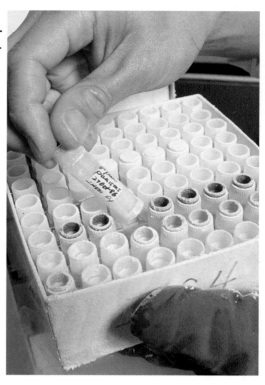

The "Frozen Zoo" is a cryogenic cell bank maintained by **CRES** that contains sperm, eggs, and **DNA** from many of the world's endangered species. These precious vials make up an ark of sorts, preserving unique genetic information for the future.

Studying the incubation of alligator eggs in the endocrinology department.

Cheetah Captive Breeding
Frozen Zoo, Etc.
Coast Horned Lizard
San Diego County Native Birds
Native Seed Bank
Native Habitat Conservation
Bighorn Sheep

NORTH AMERICA

● **Desert Tortoise**

San Clemente Island ●
Loggerhead Shrike

● **Hawaiian Forest Birds**

● **California Condor,**
Pronghorn Antelope,
Arroyo Toad

● **Mississippi Alligator**
● **Gopher Tortoise**

● **Thick-billed Parrots,**
Monarch Butterfly
Conservation Project
Leatherback & Olive ●
Ridley Sea Turtles,
Baird's Tapir

● **Caribbean Rock Iguanas**
Hawksbill Turtles
Cuban Boa

● **Harpy Eagle**

● **Giant River Otter,**
Manatee, Harpy Eagle

● **Andean Condors**

Galápagos Tortoises ●

SOUTH AMERICA

Peruvian Amazon ●
Conservation Project

● **Chacoan Peccary,**
Habitat Conservation

Our Work Around the World

Staff members of the Wild Animal Park and the San Diego Zoo are notorious for taking busman's holidays, using their vacations to work on one of many conservation field projects all over the globe. In addition to these informal conservation efforts, the Zoo, the Wild Animal Park, and CRES conduct many formal studies and projects, many in conjunction with other zoos and the governments of other countries. The map you see above highlights many of these Society-sponsored projects.

EUROPE

ASIA

● Asian Sheep

● Persian Fallow Deer

MIDDLE
EAST

Arabian Oryx ●

Lion-Tailed Macaque ●

Naryani River Pollution—
● Multiple Species

● Giant Panda, Takin,
Sclater's Monal, Chinese Monal,
Golden Monkey

● Douc Langur,
Pygmy Loris,
Slow Loris

AFRICA

● Drill

● Mountain Gorilla

● Spotted Deer, Calamian Deer,
Visayan Warty Pig

Orangutans ●
●

Komodo Dragon ●

● Guam Rail

● New Guinea Harpy Eagle,
Native Habitats,
Tree Kangaroos

Tahitian & Polynesian Lories ●

Fiji Island Banded Iguana ●

AUSTRALIA

Koala ●

● Ruffed Lemur,
Habitat Preservation

● Savanna Monitors

● Black Rhinos,
Black-footed Cat

Tuataras & Other Reptiles ●

You, as a guest at the San Diego Wild Animal Park, also help to save animals. Every dollar you spend enables us to continue our conservation work. And by learning about animals, habitats, and the importance of saving them, you too are helping to preserve our planet. ❧ The more you experience the beauty and wonder of each of these unique plants and animals, the more you can help us spread the word about working to protect them.

Birds

bee eater, northern carmine 52
bee eater, white-throated 52
bee eater, common white-fronted 53
bee eater, western blue-cheeked 53
bustard, East African kori 91
bustard, white-bellied 28
condor, California 20, 94

cotinga, spangled inside front cover
crane, East African crowned 68
crane, wattled 76
darter, African 26
falcon, northern aplomado 95
flamingo, Chilean 33
flamingo, greater 93
flamingo, lesser 93
hawk, Harris' 98
heron, black 24
heron, goliath 69
heron, great blue 29
honeycreeper, Surinam green 46
hornbill, Leadbeater's ground 78
hummingbird, western emerald 44
hummingbird, Colombian
    sparkling violet-ear 44
ibis, African sacred 93
ibis, bald 25
jacana, African 27
lapwing, long-toed 28
lorikeet, green-nape 40, 41
manakin, Guianan white-bearded 45
ostrich, South African 73
owl, burrowing 98
parrot, thick-billed 95
pelican, Eastern white 77
pelican, pink-backed 30
pygmy goose, African 27

roadrunner, western greater 97
roller, blue-bellied 28
roller, European 25
secretary bird 74
shoebill 30
starling, golden-breasted 24
stork, open-bill 26
tanager, bay-headed 47
tanager, Guianan turquoise 47
tanager, western golden-masked 47
teal, falcated 34
vulture, African white-backed 76
vulture, Ruepell's 77

Insects

ant, leafcutter 43
butterfly, birdwing 42

butterfly, blue morpho 42
butterfly, orange flame 42
butterfly, white morpho 42
scorpion, emperor 46
spider, baboon 46
stick insect, giant thorny 45
walkingstick, giant wingless 45

Mammals

addax 12
antelope, South African sable 74
babirusa 36
banteng, Javan 81
barasingha 65
blackbuck 64
bonobo 38, 86, 87
bontebok 90
buffalo, Cape 67
cheetah, South African
    12, 92, back cover
deer, axis 63
deer, Barbary red 71
deer, Mandarin sika 80
deer, Père David's 80

Plants

Reptiles

To find out more about the Wild Animal Park, the San Diego Zoo,
and the Center for Reproduction of Endangered Species (CRES),
visit our Web site at www.wildanimalpark.org,
or call (619) 231-1515 or (760) 747-8702.